BLINDFOLDED

the way to walk. the way to live.

DEDICATION

This is dedicated to the memory of…

My Grandmother, Carolyn S. Cosey. For the foundation you gave this family, upon which my life and purpose is built and has been expanded; I am eternally grateful. I hope I make you proud.

My Aunt, Judy Ann Cosey. To the best Aunt a boy could have, I say thank you. You were my friend and made me appreciate life so much. I thank you for your commitment to me and steady hand of love and support

My Father, William J. Brockenberry, Jr. "Brock". I miss you so much, Dad. So much. Thank you for being careful with the gift of your life and for giving yourself fully to your purpose. For being an example in action; selfless, supportive, strong. In doing so, you helped prompt my own purpose. I owe you everything that I have become. Thanks for being a father with a heart of The Father to me…

My Grandfather, William Brockenberry, Sr. "Brock". Thank you for your wisdom, love, and selflessness. I learned community from you and that real legacies require a focus on others for their benefit.

Until we meet again!

CONTENTS

ACKNOWLEDGMENTS

I couldn't have done this without….

My Mom. The older I get, the more I come into a fuller understanding of just how "FOR ME" you are. You are beyond the place where you have to do for me, yet you do it. Not simply because you love me, but, because you believe in what's inside of me. You were my first teacher, my best friend, and you show me Gods love in a way I couldn't have asked for. To my number one fan, thank you forever. Love you.

My Younger Brothers. Will, Dave, Dev, Dre, and Zeke; you guys have been my motivation to be great simply because I want to be an older brother in whom you can be proud. I only hope that I, in both word and deed, have shown you how much I love each of you; and that somewhere in my life, you find something that propels you to your purpose.

My Daughter, Jayde MaKenzi. I continue to strive to be my best, not for my benefit, but for you. You have made me better in every aspect of life and, thusly, deserve better of me always.

My Family. I do not know if I can capture this in words. You are my aunts and uncles, brothers and sisters, cousins and best friends. You are my second mothers and mentors, my closest frat brothers and line sisters. My Dean, my ADP, my eleven sons (Sons of Suffering-A.D.D), my mentees, my brothers from Bowie and, and my heart connections…you all are mine! We may not all be RELATED, but we are without question FAMILY, as our love runs just as deep. It is each of you who made this possible. Your generous donations to my life, in the way of love and support, as well as your selfless acts of mercy made the difference between me quitting on myself and having just enough faith to believe God for at least one more day. Your conversations, your actions, your loyalty has shown that you are committed to me. You know my worst, promote my best, and choose to love me despite my truths. You believed in me even when I didn't believe in myself and you continue to make me better by not accepting anything short of my best self. I could never repay any of you, but know that I offer my love forever.

My Extended Family. This is such a large group, I would be writing a few more pages trying to get all of you individually. But, whether you're a member of my church family at New Birth Christian Church, a member of my fraternity Phi Beta Sigma Fraternity, Incorporated (shout-out Maryland Sigmas, especially home crew Delta Mu), a member of the Bowie State University community (ayy ayy ayy ayy Bowie!), a Crusader from Riverdale Baptist, a Monarch from Ron Brown, or just a friend from one of the many arenas in which I try or have tried to keep up-I thank you. For your laughter, your support, your encouragement, your accountability, your love, your commitment, your honesty, your friendship, your kindness, your help…thanks for giving me YOU in whatever capacity you have done so. I love each of you for it and am better because of whatever your presence looks like in my life.

To My Sons. This book was finished long before God gave me either of you, but I think He waited just so I can include you in this moment. God knows I'm not perfect, and I have my own issues to manage; but, the fact that you all choose me daily and allow me to father you despite those

imperfections its truly humbling. I am so honored. I want nothing but the best for you and I struggle daily with making sure I am careful with the privilege given me. Thanks for being my sons.

My Team. Words can't at all capture the appreciation I have gained for such an amazing group of people. The love I have for you all who allow to be my most vulnerable self, without judgement, is beyond words. Your support, your counsel, your push…I see you all, and I honor each of you.

My Young Kings. I hope someday you can remember me with fondness, confident that my intentional interactions with you all were rooted in love and unwavering belief in your greatest self. May this inspire you to find your best self and not to be afraid or intimidated by who he is. Here's to the faith needed to becme that person with ease.

INTRODUCTION

In August 2014, I had the opportunity to speak at my home church, New Birth Christian of Suitland, MD and the topic was something regarding "faith". I referenced the story of Peter's water-walking experience to illustrate all of my points (*Matthew 14*). The next day, I went to work and, very clearly started to hear the spirit of God say to me *"get out of the boat"*. Now, up until this point, I had grown very 'blah' with life. I believed that God did a lot for me and I desired a lot for myself, even; but life had dealt some pretty devastating blows and I was extremely unfulfilled and uninspired. I remembered the words that people had spoken into my life, over my life; prophecies. I thought about the gifts that were present in my life; the talents. Then I saw where I was, and how none of those things seemed to be producing anything worth talking about (that is nothing that could rekindle the fire). I didn't feel passionate about life anymore. And no, it wasn't that I wanted to die, however the fire for living was slowly, but certainly, losing its heat. Until this point, I never really understood how people became stuck. Or how they moved from passion to passive, from living to merely existing. Yet, here I was, dim. Here, I was them. Nothing was giving me a reason to flame, and I started to accept the place in which I existed as the place where I would ultimately die.

Weeks went by and I kept hearing God say "get out of the boat". I even started posting little nuggets for life and living relative to faith with the hashtag **#getouttheboat** on all my social media outlets; but, I wrestled with what that instruction meant for me. You see, the more I remained in the situation, the more I started to realize just how miserable I had become. And, I thought it was just the job, but this was about much more than that. I had a good job, made decent money, and honestly wasn't even working that hard. It was easy, but I was miserable. It was as though my internal levees had broken and I was being emotionally flooded with waves of feelings to which I had grown numb. This current lot in life was my boat. The complacency. The frustration. The doubt. The resolve that this was it…this was my boat…and this was the moment I realized I had to make a decision: either get out or get stuck.

I wanted more than anything to believe that every idea and thought for what God wanted of my life still had a chance to be. I wanted to be done with the place and perception of life I had grown used to. I was exhausted with trying to hold up my emotions and I needed to get out of the boat for the sake of my life. I believed God was calling me not simply from a job, but from that place in which I had started to settle. In order to see his outcomes for my life, to live as He had destined, and to see the fruition of Jeremiah 29:11 come to pass; I had to walk away from where I was physically, emotionally and spiritually. My life, in that condition, could not produce any of God's outcomes. As Proverbs teaches, we are as we think. Our outcomes are a product of our mindsets; and my mindset was one of defeat. All I wanted was to live a life fulfilled, to be the best me possible…whatever that meant, whatever that looked like. This wasn't about writing a book, this wasn't about getting rich, this wasn't about becoming famous. This was about fulfilling a life of purpose and seeing the product of my potential made real. I had no idea what would happen next...but, I had to get out of the boat.

Before you begin the task of reading this book, I need you to commit to something first: Your Best You. You will hear me refer to this idea of "YOUR BEST YOU" often throughout this book, so we should probably get in agreement to what I mean.

While I understand that it sounds good, our best often goes underachieved. As we travel our road in life, it is imperative we become our best selves in pursuit of our raison d'etre. I am convinced that the reason we live is much bigger than us, and that in the grand scheme of it all, we are interconnected with the lives of legacies of others. The impact of a life of purpose sets waves of influence in motion that are far reaching through time, generation, and moments. Self-discovery and identity doesn't happen isolated of others and, therefore, who we become is largely shaped by the condition of those we had access to, and ultimately will be part of the molding of those who have access to us. This is what the phrasing doing the "best with what I have" is alluding to. In short, people can more readily become their best selves, produce their best works, dream their best dreams and give their best efforts when they are provided with the best of others demonstrated similarly.

So, what does 'my best me' even look like? I got you because I know you asked. This is a hard question, even for as simple as it may seem. I believe it's difficult because the idea of "best" is pretty much subjective. My son and I were having what you could call a "passionate presenting of personal perspectives" (alliteration heavy!) and at the nexus of the points discussed was this idea that his definition of "best" and mine were unaligned. Human nature with all of our agency, and rights, and free will would lead us to feel that determining best is certainly left up to the primary user of a thing or, in our case, SELF. However, I think that while SELF could be the determinant, the right to name what is best isn't based on the primary user. I would suggest that the right to define the "best" of a thing should be reserved for that which holds the most unbiased knowledge of said thing. So, in the middle of the argu- I mean, passionate presenting of personal perspectives I was having with my son, I was able to remind him that he only knows what he wants to know, and even that information could be skewed. LOL. Seriously, though, think about it. When you get a new car, you don't know all the features and perks unless you have otherwise learned them from someone who could be considered an expert in the matter (creative/design team member, committed and honest salesperson, professional who reviews new automobiles, etc.). You get a new phone, even the manufacturer walks you through its latest features during the set up. You see, we are okay with yielding our own 'right of determination' to the vision and knowledge of another when it comes to anything else. But self, no- we are adamant that we know us best because we are the primary users. And, look, maybe you do; I'm not even here to argue. I only want us to be on the same page when it comes to this so you can get the most from the remainder of this book, and my efforts.

But, to determine best, one simply has to understand capacity. Best happens when effort meets capacity. There was a different time when my son and I were having another "discussion of deductions", where in response to my supposition that he was being mediocre, he retorted that he was "trying his best". And, in true form of self, I disagreed and offered him the following visual. With my left hand, I grabbed a simple bottle of water, what's that about 12 ounces or so? Then, with my right hand, I picked up a larger, empty juice container, about 30 ounces, and here's what I said:

"This water bottle is full. It, within it's twelve ounce capacity to hold liquid, is doing so at maximal capacity. It is doing the BEST it was designed to do. However, if I took this same water bottle which in the context of its 12-ounce capacity is operating at its best, and I dumped it into this juice container, it wouldn't even be half full. (I gave it a dramatic pause, it's always good for point making with the teens). This is you, son. Two years ago, you were this water bottle. Your capacity was smaller. So, the effort that you are giving now, may have been your best TWO YEARS AGO. But, see, son, you've grown in two years. Your capacity has increased. You have had years of development, challenge of ideology, shifts in perspective, provocation of thoughts, maturity; you have grown and so your capacity isn't that of two years ago. So, when your capacity grows, your efforts must also grow to keep up with where you are now capable. Otherwise, you give me 12-ounce effort for 30-ounce

capacity, and the same effort that once was deemed best, is now become mediocre. "

What am I saying? Your best you is the you that results from a consistent engagement with life wherein capacity is stretched beyond it's current limit, and subsequently, effort is also stretched in order to try to meet that capacity. Here's the real: you will, or should, always be chasing your best self. Let me say that again and add… you should always be chasing your BEST SELF, not racing your PAST SELF. Every single day, life offers us the opportunity to grow in capacity, with its lessons, pains, successes, relationships, interactions, challenges, wins, losses- and everything in between. If we engage these opportunities- not run away from them, or ignore them; not settle or throw them aside- but engage them to work on and in us- we position ourselves for maximum output. That, my friend, is all I want to ask you to commit to before you read. Because without faith, you choose to remain in the place you stand and will surrender your future to the thief that wears the mask of complacency, mediocrity, and "good enough".

DEAR READER,

I sit here, staring at a blank screen and I have no idea of what I want to say. I am filled with so many thoughts. I know I am supposed say something. I want to say something; I just don't know what. I laugh, to cover fear and inhibitions, and I question even my right to speak to you. Who am I to say anything to you? I am conflicted within myself because while I feel I have something worth sharing, I wonder if anyone else would find the value in my words. No, I am not an "expert" in any field. No, behind my name you will not find any respectable combination of letters. At the point of me writing even this paragraph, I was without a college degree, living in a basement, late on my rent, without car insurance, waiting on two court dates for driving on a suspended license, with about $7 to my entire name. Why, I ask myself, would you care to listen to anything I have to say?

These are all the same things I asked God and therein lay my issue made evident. Since I was younger, I have struggled with my self-confidence so much so that I literally doubted my performance in almost everything I tried to do. I fail to find belief in myself, and I saw it show up as a hinderance in my interactions and my successes. Instead, like many others, I allow my current state of being (usually heightened in the flawed perspectives and lofty self-expectations) dictate and define what can be. But sometimes, just sometimes, you have to stop listening to all the reasons that disqualify you. Sometimes you have to look at the standard from a different perspective, maybe even institute a completely different standard, altogether. The truth is many of us wrestle in our faith often because we are still wrestling within ourselves. We are at war trying so hard to believe that we can be anywhere near close to what God says we can be and who He says we are. It's about time for me, and maybe you as well, to gain a new perspective. Perspective, or how we see something, affects how we purpose something in our minds. And we all know that as a man thinks, so is he (Proverbs 23:7).

Now, let me give you a fair disclaimer. This book is not an attempt at a theological exegesis about faith. If you're looking for a philosophical, theoretical exposition, you probably won't find that here. I am also not even remotely interested in giving you a few sermons or flood you with familiar church colloquialisms. This book may not challenge your intellect or rock your world with statements of revelation and profundity. All this author intends to offer you is a different perspective. Every line, every word- all that I have to give you is simply what God gave me.

This is a journey for me. It's a journey in faith that has stretched me in extension of where I was comfortable and with what was convenient. It is an exploration in faith that pushed me to my limits and then said, "go further", redefining what those limits were. Every chapter is filled with lessons that I've learned along this road. Inside of each you will find moments of vulnerability in what has been one of the most terrifying points of my life. These pages are packed with heartfelt emotions and transparency, all raw and without filter. There were times in living this that I was overwhelmed with so many feelings that I wanted nothing to do with chronicling it. You're getting all of that. You're going to get moments when I felt like quitting, as well as times when I felt I was sinking and being smothered under the weight of it all. This was undoubtedly one of the hardest things I have ever had to do. This book is so much more than just the normal conversations had about faith. As I mentioned before, this is all perspective driven.

1.   Writing this book was CHALLENGING.

The times were hard, the lessons harder…and to live through them with enough energy left to write about it; that, too, was tough. To know you can't quit because God may just be using your life as an example or teaching point for someone else; tough. To know that you've got to be vulnerable and honest, open and transparent, all while trying to be encouraging; tough. I wasn't sure that I was justified in what I was doing. Here I am arguing with God daily about my situation, and then coming to you to tell you how to make it through yours. I felt like a hypocrite. So, for a short period of time, I just stopped writing. The document was unopened on my computer for almost two months. The challenge of trying to make sense of a process to which I was a slave was overbearing. I wanted no parts.

I initially blamed the hiatus on my "lack of inspiration". God wasn't speaking and, subsequently, I didn't feel compelled to write. **LIES!** The truth was I lacked discipline, and where there is no discipline there will also be no faith and vice versa. Think about it. It's very hard to remain disciplined to a process that makes you uncomfortable and that you don't enjoy. It's even harder to stay disciplined to a process where you may not see the results immediately or when they aren't as obvious; a process that you may not even understand. Think about how many people give up on counseling or dieting or working out. They either don't believe enough in the process or practitioner to commit; or they try to get around it, by committing to results without putting in the effort. That's what faith requires of us- believing to the point of doing in spite of what I UNDERSTAND, what I SEE, or what I FEEL.

In addition to all of that, writing this also made me look introspectively at my own "stuff". Whether or not we choose to admit it, we all have our "stuff". You know, the things you don't want to deal with or be dealt with about. At some point in our lives in order to grow beyond our current selves, we must first confront and get over the things that hold us bound to those conditions. This starts with admitting that we've got some stuff. After this, we must then make the conscious effort of sorting through and dealing with the stuff that we've been ignoring for years. That's not always comfortable, if it ever is.

2.   This process was CONFRONTATIONAL.

Most people I know don't really care for confrontation and will usually try to avoid it at all costs. The road of faith will cause you to confront and be confronted by some realities that you just don't want to face. It's going to bring to the forefront the truths of your innermost fears, inhibitions, and hang-ups. You will have to face your ugliness and your brokenness. Faith can only go as far as our baggage allows and, the issue with that is, not everything is allowed on the journey. It's like traveling, not everything can go on the trip. Some things you will have to check and leave with security. Some attitudes and mindsets are holding your faith back from its fullest development. Some of you have scaled back, or completely given up hope in the dreams and visions you had for your own life. Some have even allowed your fears and past failures to dictate the range of your faith. You have placed limitations and boundaries on your belief based on the systems and social structures of people. In doing so, you have made God smaller and restricted the possibilities of His promises for, His power in, and His plans concerning your life. The audacity of you to tell God that He's thinking too big of you, that He's planned to great for you, or that He's expecting too much of you. However, we do it every time we refuse to act in faith. You may as well just be saying "NO GOD, YOU'RE WRONG ABOUT ME!"

3. The process of writing this was also COMFORTING.

Now, as uncomfortable as I was, I realized this was my plight and I was stuck here. I know we like to think we have a choice all the time, but let's be real; we don't. Even when I wanted to choose to just go get a job that I knew shouldn't be working, or go do something that I knew I shouldn't do; it never panned out. When I tell you God exercised complete sovereignty in this situation, the only way to remove myself from the plan was stop living-which was not an option. He shut every door that had been shut, and opened every door that had been opened. He made every way that was made. Nothing I wanted to do was done outside of

God's privileged power. Nothing. While it was frustrating, it was very comforting to know that this process was in His total control. If nothing else, I knew that I was in God's hand and right in the middle of whatever plan He had (though sometimes I acted as if I had completely forgotten that). I didn't know the plan, and yes, sometimes the pressure of the process invoked an emotionally driven response. No, it wasn't comfortable but, at the end of every day, behind every fit I threw, and underneath every frustrated breath I took; I wanted to believe I would be okay.

I don't know where you are in your faith. Some of you may not even be faith-driven people. That's fine, too. However, whether you are faith-oriented or not, my hope is that the pages of this book cause you to be ignited (or reignited) in the pursuit of YOUR BEST YOU. And know that no one has ever become their best without going BEYOND their own strength, pushing BEYOND their own limits, connecting BEYOND their own SPACES, and doing something BEYOND their own comfort. I pray that the best of you won't settle for living in your current situation, but will take the risk of trusting BEYOND what you can see, to step out into a world of endless possibilities and powerful purpose. I hope that you will be *challenged*, because without such there can be no growth. I hope that you will be *confronted* by truths that you have hidden and ignored for years, and by unfulfilled dreams and passions that have been neglected. I pray that you will be *comforted* through your process with the knowledge and power of God's sovereignty, beyond the frustration and exhaustion, and beyond the anger and desire to quit or remain.

I hope that in my journey, you can find something for yours that makes the promises of God worth believing and holding on to. I pray that you will read something that inspires you to **PUSH BEYOND** your place of ordinary faith, into a realm of redefined limitations. I pray that you're able to look into yourself and **SEE BEYOND** the reality you've created and, with some honesty, find those hidden things that have stifled you and hindered the move of God as intended in and for your life. I hope that you will **GROW BEYOND** your current level of worship and obedience, where your decisions concerning your relationship with God are dependent on nothing outside of who He is. And, if nothing else, I sincerely desire for you to experience a new level of faith, what I believe is the true faith; uninhibited, unrestrained, and unlimited. If faith for you is not a way of life, then what is? If there is no faith, on what grounds do you have for expectation? What is there to hope for? Whatever you do, however you choose to live, just LIVE! Don't die in the boat if there is life to be lived out on the water. Time to WALK!

Take note: You will find some song references in the book. I think it's amazing how God will give us songs for the season in which we find ourselves, or even songs that speak directly to the moment or the lesson He's allowing us to experience. You've been there, I'm sure, where a song you've heard time and time again all of a sudden is resonating so deeply in your spirit that it's as if you're hearing it for the first time. That's God. Truth is: there were times during this journey where I was one song away from quitting, throwing in another towel, and walking away from God. Some of you have your own song of this season, or songs to go with the lessons that God is using life to teach you. Sing them. Sing them loudly, and sing them daily. Don't let them escape your heart until the next one comes. It helps, I'm sure of it. I've included these in order to give you a deeper connection to my experience. As you live this out for yourself, take note of the songs God gives you in the moments.

I've also added some questions and statement for help stir thoughts and cause you to reflect as you read. The more we involve our faculties in the process of learning, the more our learning remains with us. I encourage you to read this with a journal next to you, so that you can capture any of your own contemplations that may take root in your heart or mind. And, get all your thoughts out, read them and read them again. This is a simple read, but take your time with it. Process it, chew on it, digest it. This is food.

Finally, may my journey and its lessons inspire you to achieve greater things, experience greater places, and become the greater no, greatest, you. Let this experience push you to find the courage and the will to get out of your proverbial boat and walk upon the water to wherever you're being called. There is so much beyond where you are, who you are…what you are; and you won't see it, until you learn to live blindfolded!

In His Love and Service,

Dawaine Marques Cosey

Lesson and Listen- "Oceans" Hillsong

1- (RE)DEFINING *FAITH*

Faith is much too complex of a thing for my mind to even try to simplify. So I won't even try. It's dynamic and multifaceted. The more I walk it out, the more it baffles and amazes me. I think that is how it is designed to work, though. Faith operates against every humanistic instinct which seems to come more natural to us. It works oppositional to our intelligence, reasoning, logic, and emotions…every aspect of us that makes and justifies our existence as human beings is contested in the practice of faith.

So what exactly is faith and why is it so essential to the life of any believer? The word of God teaches that Christ is "author and finisher of our faith" (Hebrews 12:2). In other words, our ability and privilege to demonstrate faith, as we know it, started with (and requires) Christ. It says that 'to as many as believed in him he gave the power to become the sons of God' (John 1:12). Accepting Christ, the author of our faith, the hope of glory within us, gives us access to the privilege of hope by connecting to the power it takes to become. I mean, what would hope be without a chance or an opportunity?

To put it plainly, faith is critical to a believer because it is the system upon which we were made to live. It's what the Windows 2010 is to the computer; not merely a program on the machine, but it's the operating system which provides a base on which to establish and build the programs, operate software, and demonstrate its full potential. Faith is not merely belief, but true faith goes beyond belief to the point of INVITING that in which you believe to become INVOLVED in detailed aspects of your life from a position of INFLUENCE. From that influence, we gain the INSIGHT, INSTRUCTION, and INSPIRATION of that source. Through these, we are educated, encouraged and empowered to become or to do in accordance with the will of the entity in which said faith was placed. Look at it like this: when most of us are lost, we use our GPS. Whether it's on our phone or programmed in our vehicles, we have faith in this mapping system to help us find our way to our destination. So, we type in our destinations and we follow whatever the directions are given us by way of the GPS. This is a perfect example of the operation of faith by our definition. We believe in the accuracy of the GPS so much that we *invite* it to be *involved* in this aspect of our trip from a position of *influence*. That influence gives us the power in the way of insight and instructions to get out of our lost situation and find our way to the desired destination. That's how faith works and this is why John 1:12 includes that critical line "as many as received Him", or for everyone who gave Him the room to be involved, He then gave them POWER (insight, instructions, inspiration) to become. And, by power, we aren't just simply talking ability, but ability by way of decision and control.

The destination of our lives, the access to become or to do that in which God has destined for your life or moment in your life rests upon your decisions in faith. Faith gives us the opportunity to become more than we are or to do more than we've ever done by choosing to make the decision to believe. Faith empowers us with all we need to move BEYOND our "what is" into the possibilities and outcomes of "what can be" in the one with whom ALL THINGS are possible.

Faith is a LIFE THING. When you live a life built from this kind of faith, you live based on a belief and interaction with God that invites and involves him in every aspect. Your decisions. Your thoughts. Your words. Your priorities. Your money. Your goals. Your aspirations. Your dreams. Your ambitions. Your dark places. Your fears. Your secrets. Your inhibitions, hang-ups and holdups. Your insecurities. If you want God's insight in your life, then your life and every aspect therein should be open to God's involvement. A life of faith must allow God the influence in and beyond all these aspects into the very fabric of who we are. This is the type of faith we were created to exhibit. This is the kind that God loves and responds to. For it is when our lives are open to God's involvement and lived under God's influence that He is pleased. It's from that openness that He is able to produce his promises and His will for our lives. God does not want to leave us in the condition that the world and our experiences therein have created for us or confined us to. It pleases Him to see us open; for it is in such openness that He is able to heal where we've been hurt, build us where we've been torn down, make whole where we've been shattered, and love us where we've been neglected; making all things work for our good. Faith is one of the greatest gifts that God has lavished upon us and, when in operation, offers a consistent demonstration of God's commitment to His children. It is through faith that we are saved and even salvation was given to us as a result of an act of faith. (Hebrews 12:2).

When you want God's outcomes, you must examine the extent of God's involvement; which means you must examine the extent of your invitation. So, the question is WHERE IS YOUR FAITH? If your faith hasn't stretched you to see BEYOND your NOW, it's not faith. If your faith hasn't allowed you believe that you are not confined to the limitations of any reality, then it's not faith. Without faith, life can never produce God's ABUNDANCE; the manner in which He has secured and designed it for you. By not exercising true faith, we subsequently make the choice to void the gift of Christ's life- the same life which authors our faith, the faith which substantiates our hope. Instead of being the "more than overcomers" through Christ Jesus, we choose to live at the mercy of life's circumstances and situations.

Faith is how we conquer and how we defeat. It's not only process and product of belief, but it's literally the cause of that belief. Faith is what keeps us going when everything around us gives us reason to quit. Faith is what keeps us holding on and hanging tough when the odds are against us. Faith is what keeps us in the fight when we feel like we've been knocked down for the count. Faith is what makes us love beyond our hurt and give beyond our rejections. Faith is what allows us to forgive without grudges and to endure without complaining. Faith is what leads us to make decisions that don't seem logical to the natural eye. What is faith? It is the process that brings out the best in you and gives your potential access to possibilities. And, no, this process doesn't come without opposition. The opponents to this true faith are all housed within some aspects of who we are. Whether it's fear or past failures, pride or insecurities; this opposition is found inside part of our personality, past trauma, or even present issue. God brings about the external circumstances of life to challenge us in the places of whatever that opposition is so that we have the opportunity to conquer it and develop the faith to become better, more complete versions of ourselves. It all starts with you making a decision to trust that process. It will be tough, but it's worth it. Your future, your past, yourself…it's all worth it!

Your best you should be your only option.

Time to READ
<u>R</u>EFLECTION <u>E</u>VALUATION <u>A</u>DMISSION <u>D</u>ECISION

R-eflection

What situation/s currently active or that have gone unresolved in your life that may need some faith? What opposition (internal and/or external) are you facing right now? Why do you think you are facing this kind of opposition?

E-valuation

Compare and evaluate our working definition of FAITH as explained in chapter 1 with what you've previously understood and accepted it to be. Do the two collide, connect, or other collaborate?

A-dmission

Which part of our definition do you find the most difficult with engaging in your life? Why is so hard for you to implement this? With this definition in mind, in whom or what have you placed your faith? How has this worked for you?

D-ecision

What things need to happen in your life (and within your control) and what action steps will you take towards those directives in order for you to activate true faith and see YOUR BEST YOU?!

2- SEEING BEYOND *THE PROMISE*

In order to really understand faith, one must have an adequate comprehension of hope. The two are dependent upon one another, and they both work together in the process of you becoming your best self. To illustrate the relationship, let me use the idea of air.

Air is pretty cool, wouldn't you say? It is all around us, filling all available space; and, yet, it goes unseen. We know air is there not because it makes itself known through some loud, flashy display, but because of the mere presence of other things that rely on its existence. It is the thing that gives life to our very being, for without it we can't live. Through us, so many great things can be accomplished, so many amazing things can be done; but, it all starts with air. We can feel it; it moves us. It can push us. If you can understand the concept of air, you can understand how this faith thing works, as well. See, hope is a lot like air. We know it is there, but it must be substantiated with something more. Enter FAITH.

Faith is the substance of my hope and the evidence of what I do not see (Hebrews 11:1). Hope is invisible until it is materialized by faith. Think of it like a balloon. While air can't be seen naturally as itself, we are able to see proof of its existence when we inflate a balloon. This is true of hope and faith. If hope is the invisible, intangible air that gives us life and keeps us going, then faith is the balloon that gives it evidence. In short, if we have hope, we must also have faith to prove it.

1. Faith is a reflection of our HOPE.

Every move we make in faith is ultimately motivated by the strength of our hope. There can be no inflated balloon if there is no air given thereto. So, faith is a reflection of our hope in that it produces visible and sometimes tangible evidence of the invisible action which is our belief.

Hope, then, is important to the validity and activity of faith and, more often than not, when we encounter issues in our faith, we really expose an issue with our hope. When hope is threatened, intimidated, or removed, it decreases the visibility of our displays of faith and diminishes the possibility of faith being put into action. Often times the problem with correctly walking by faith is simply a matter of *misplaced hope*. For many of us, we are putting more hope in the promise instead of the promiser. We have become so enamored with the "what is coming" that we often forget to consider the "who is bringing it". Here's what wrong with that. When we forget about who promised something and instead focus on what was promised, we set ourselves up for imminent failure.

2. A promise is only as good as the one who promises it.

As in the case of the boy who cried wolf, we don't too frequently believe the one whose integrity or character is found to be questionable. For this reason, we cannot afford to disconnect the promise from the promiser; and, if the integrity of the promiser is at all questionable, it heightens our chances of being greatly disappointed. Faith has to extend beyond the promise onto the promiser, otherwise we will continue to find ourselves in this cycle of disappointed hope.

The bible teaches us in Proverbs 13:12 that "hope deferred makes the heart sick" and we know that from the heart flow the issues of life (Proverbs 4:23). When our faith doesn't extend beyond the promise on to the promiser, we will always find ourselves in the place of disappointment which robs us of our desire to hope. When our heart is robbed of its hope, our life reflects a hopeless condition. Many of us have misplaced our hope, and we have been disappointed so many times that we've now come to expect it. It's psychological. We've convinced ourselves that it hurts less when you expect it, so we've learned to do just that: EXPECT IT. We walk around, hopeless, and the only expectation we have of life is to disappoint us. We expect people to fail us; we expect things to not work out. We are always anticipating something to go wrong, and when it does, no matter how small it may have been, we refuse to move past it. We become numb. But, just because you stop feeling the anguish behind the disappointment, doesn't mean it stops producing some devastating effects. Like for instance, if you hit my arm, I'll feel it. Keep hitting it, and eventually it'll numb up and I'll stop feeling it. But keep hitting it, and though I may no longer feel it due to its numbness, a bruise will form and the muscle underneath will undoubtedly be negatively affected. What I am saying is that some of us have been let down in our hope so much, that we don't even have what it takes to acknowledge the pain anymore. Our lack of faith and our failure to act in faith has nothing to do with our balloon and everything to do with our air. This is why we are reminded by the writer in Hebrews 10:23, "let us hold tightly without wavering to the hope we affirm, for God can be trusted to keep his promise."

In addition to this, we must also have the faith that goes beyond our promise onto the promiser because:

3. The responsibility of the promise is always assumed by its promiser.

When we disconnect one (the promise) from the other (the promiser), we end up with a condition I call "Performance Transferal". Performance Transferal is what occurs when the responsibility of the performance is transferred from one agent to another. Remember, the responsibility to perform a promise is naturally that of the one by whom it promised. When God gives us a promise, it isn't to get us to chase after it, but to encourage us to chase after HIM. He who holds the promise is actually more important than the promise itself, for they are the one who has custody of it. However, when we disconnect promise from promiser and put our faith in just one and not the other, said responsibility now becomes assumed by the one who received the promise-YOU.

Has God ever promised you something and instead of waiting for Him to move and confirm, you took over based solely of the excitement of the potential? God promises us a spouse and so we start to make future plans with the first guy or girl that walks in our path. We try to make it work, just because it looks like it fits. Sometimes, we try to force something that isn't or make it fit when it doesn't even seem to do so naturally. This is an example of Performance Transferal. I did this all the time. When I quit my job back in October 2014, I initially believed that God had something greater in store for me, you know, something fulfilling that was connected to my purpose. That believe came with the promise that He would sustain me until it manifested. However, I quit and immediately started looking for other jobs. I would need something part-time, that paid some livable wage and that would hold me over. Then the spirit reminded me that I had literally just left something part-time, paying extremely well, that could've held me over. So, what was it I looking for? I left, trusting God, only to put myself right back in the same situation?

This is a perfect example of Performance Transferal. I was trying to sustain myself because I had separated the promise of being sustained from the promiser, God. As I mentioned in earlier, I knew God wanted me to "get out of the boat". But, subconsciously, I started focusing on what I needed to do to stay atop the water, instead of focusing on the one who called me out upon the water to begin with. Whenever we find ourselves focused on the situation surrounding the promise, it is very easy to slip into panic mode. When we have taken on the wrong focus and thus the responsibility of the promise, the greatness of the promise, once perceived by us, is met with a skeptic reality based upon the realization of our limitations. Since we are not the ones who promised it, we clearly did not possess the power or perspective to perform it on our own. Otherwise, wouldn't it have already been done? When you take the promiser out of the equation but keep the promise, you assume the responsibility of bringing said promise to pass. Since the promise is usually greater than your immediate ability to perform it, the connected responsibility usually demands more than you are capable of giving, causing stress and turmoil to take up residence where God intended to bring peace.

Performance Transferal also takes place when we refuse to allow God's involvement in aspects of our life. Again, faith should lead us to see and believe beyond our own limitations. However, when we don't operate in faith with the belief that moves us to invoke God's involvement, influence, and insight, it usually results in our attempt to make things happen by our own resources. If we don't have God's insight in our lives, we are trapped to our own ignorance. We only have a very limited perception of what's going on at any given time, and we take actions birthed from those perceptions. Without insight from God, or more full perspective, we can mistakenly perceive what is truly preparation for the promise as permanent punishment and prevention from the promise. And this is usually where it all goes bad. When we have purposed something for ourselves in our own hearts, we will try to find a way around anything that gets in our way of having it.

This kind of Performance Transferal is found in Genesis 16. Remember, Sarai (Sarah) hadn't bore any children to Abram (Abraham) at this point, as the bible tells us she was unable to do so. The bible says "and Sarai said to Abram 'behold now, the Lord has prevented me from bearing children. Go in to my servant; *it*

may be that I shall obtain children by her (16:1-2)". Look at what happens after Sarai decided to act from the limited, ignorant perception of her condition, without God's involvement and insight. The bible says "Sarai, Abram's wife took Hagar the Egyptian, her servant, and gave her to Abram her husband as a wife. And he went in to Hagar and she conceived. And when she saw that she had conceived, she looked with contempt on her mistress. And Sarai said to Abram, 'May the wrong done to me be on you! (16-3:5). Now, isn't this wild. Sarai, looking through the sight of her reality, conceives the plan, and then carries it out of her own power- all of which is restricted. She goes so far as to present her servant to her husband in order to FORCE the promise to take place. Once the plan produces the "results", she immediately feels the sting of her actions and is thrown into a place of guilt, hurt, wrongdoing, blame…and who knows what else. Have you ever done something like this, gone out of your way just to get in your way? What if I told you that sometimes we create our own plights because we birthed something in our life that was never meant to exist. We have constructed intentional accidents, purposed mistakes, deliberate disasters all around us; and because they weren't designed to exist in the first place, we are thrown into fires that we may not have been equipped to withstand…like depression, guilt, mental warfare. It may sound extreme, but I'm telling you it's real. If you ever been tortured by internal tensions and anxieties, things that keep you up at night, that weigh you down at the mere sight of them; it may have been the unnatural result of perverted promise.

Our lives are either lived based on God's insight or our own ignorance. Every action we take comes from a place of influence and operates from some place of perspective. When you only live from your ignorance, or what you don't know, you will never understand as God understands or see as He sees. Without God's insight, you will torment yourself with what you create through the failed attempts at trying to figure it out alone. It is imperative that when God gives us the promise, we pursue HIM not IT. Though the promise can be God sent, it can become a God-block if we make it more important than He is. There is a reason Christ tells us to "Seek ye first the kingdom of God and his righteousness…" (Matthew 6:33). It is in God's presence where you will find God's promise. It is crazy to think, but we can absolutely miss what's promised if we become more driven to it than to its holder. If we are only concerned with the details of a promise, then all it will take is a better detail of some other promise to pull us in a different direction. Remember, the enemy is not short on attractive details. If you are not intentional and careful in your pursuit, you will end up giving chase to an attractive promise that's being controlled by an enemy of God, and thus, an enemy of your destiny.

Pursue the presence and person of God, and His promises that are connected to you will meet you there.

Time to READ
REFLECTION EVALUATION ADMISSION DECISION

R-eflection

What initial thoughts and/or emotions did you encounter while reading this chapter? Name and explore them in connection with this idea of misplaced hope.

E-valuation

How has the result of a heart made sick, that is unfulfilled hope, affected your ability to host and capacity to believe expectation? Where has this thwarted hope shown up consistently in your life and how may it have affected your outlook and disposition in those areas? Do you feel it has held you back in any way possible from demonstrating faith?

A-dmission

When and with what have you been guilty of Performance Transferal? What situations in your life are a result of you trying to force a promise into existence? Which details did you "see" present in your reality played a part to your opting to attempting to make something happen?

D-ecision

What things need to happen in your life (and within your control) and what action steps will you take towards those directives in order for you to hope again?

3- SEEING BEYOND *PLANS*

So, I have an issue. In my life, I have had to learn to become a planner. I hate it, really; but, I've had to learn (albeit grudgingly) to do so. Unless it's something of interest, I'm just not one of those planning types. However, I do understand the need for plans. As the old adage says, "if you fail to plan, you plan to fail". And, I guess maybe there is some truth in that. It is for that reason that many of us are strict planners because, as we've had to learn, failure is a bitter taste that we would rather avoid. So we make our plans. We map out our lives while freshmen in college; when we will marry, when we will have children, and even where we will live. We structure our professional lives as we graduate and start our careers. I've known some people who are so busy that they have to have every single minute of their day scheduled in a planner, because there's just that much going on in their lives. Listen, I'm not saying there's anything wrong with any of this. I sometimes wish I could be more of this detail-oriented, "know exactly what's going to happen" type of person, myself. I am an advocate of plans. They assist us in making the most efficient use of our time; help us to reach our goals by acting as guides; and, more importantly, they teach us to be prepared and thus, in control of situations that may go awry. It is here where much of faith goes to contest: CONTROL.

The lack of faith often stems from a deeper human issue. That issue: the fear of losing [a sense of] control. The act of faith will often require you to relinquish the control in which planning allows you to maintain. Let's be honest, we all like control. Who doesn't enjoy having a handle over things, situations, or even, people for some? I know I do (not the people part). The more control we have in a situation, the more confident we are in said situation. It's like watching a horror movie, which I have to admit, I used to be a huge fan of. (When I say used to, I mean currently am). The first time you see the film, everything makes you jump. Every scare that was designed to be frightening is just that. Sometimes, even those things that weren't supposed to be scary do the trick, but I digress. I, like a lot of the men I know, would use horror movies as a component to gain some leverage in my dating life. My logic, though juvenile, made a lot of sense. The girl, if you could convince her to go, would be nervous, jumping in terror the entire time, which allowed you the justifiable reason needed to nestle her into the safety of your maybe "not so manly" arms (this worked best in high school/early college). To ensure that I could pull this off, I had a foolproof system that would make certain I wouldn't be as jumpy or as afraid as my date. I would first go see the movie alone, usually around midday when the theatre was empty. This way, I could jump and shout like a baby all I needed to with no risk of embarrassment. By the time I went out on the date, I was in complete control of my reactions because I knew what was going to happen and when. So, while my date was flinching around and throwing her face into her hands, I was braced and prepared for the impending fright, so to seem completely unmoved by the film's best attempt to scare us. See, acts of faith challenge those systems that often constitute your self-centered confidence, creating an unnerving disturbance in the level of comfort you have while "walking it out". In other words, acts of faith can be just as scary, unsettling, and nerve-wrecking as watching that film for the first time. They have the unique ability to invoke panic and worry because they nullify our source of confidence (planning/preparation) which encourages mental and emotional sobriety and calm.

When God told me to leave my job in August 2014, I was not with it! (I'm sorry y'all, I didn't agree with the plan at all) However, I started to become more comfortable with the idea of leaving my job the more I realized that I would have a hand of control in the situational circumstances that would likely arise. I had a check coming in which would afford me the opportunity to secure my rent payments into the New Year. After which time, I would have another one coming that would cover me for a few more months of financial responsibility. See, this is the normal reaction of most of us. It becomes a lot easier to trust God in "faith" as long as we have a plan that allows us to self-sustain throughout the act. We say "Okay, God. I'll quit my job because I have the money to take care of things", as if we are doing him a favor by exercising faith. Once I quit, I was almost arrogant in what God had told me to do. However, after a few months, emergencies popped up and money started running low. Wouldn't you know it, just like me, I went right back into panic mode. I started questioning again if I was sure He told me to leave the job in the first place, simply because my plan to sustain myself had come undone. Whenever our "following God" is dependent upon resources that promote self-reliance, excuse my language but WE AIN'T FOLLOWING GOD. Instead, we are telling God "I like your plan, but you can't do it without my help."

One of the most popular ways that we demonstrate lack of faith in God is:

1. We demand for plans ahead of time.

We want to plan out our days; we want to plan out our future. We love planning, even when we fail to do it. Plans involve details, and when we are not privy to the details of something, especially that in which we are involved, we are made to feel powerless over it. The question then becomes, are you okay with being powerless?

I once did this demonstration while preaching. Look at it like this: You're in an auditorium listening to a speaker. He calls you on stage, which has a platform about five feet above the ground, and blindfolds you. While you are blindfolded, he spins you around and moves you to the edge of the stage with your back facing the crowd. So there you are, without the ability to see and slightly confused due to the spinning, with your heels hanging over the edge of the five foot high stage and the speaker then tells you to fall back. What do you do?

You would be crazy to fall back. While five feet isn't much when we can see it, it's dangerously scary when we can't. So you don't move. As a matter of fact, you secure your footing even more. (This is what happened when I performed this at my church.) What the speaker didn't tell you is that he had previously arranged for some pretty strong and solid guys to walk up once you were blindfolded. He didn't tell you that they were told to be prepared to catch you when you fell. But you never fell. I really believe this is how God orchestrates our lives around his asks of us in faith. See, what we have to realize is that we are not always going to know how God is going to work it out, but we have to trust that He sees what we don't see. Since He gave us the instruction, we must know that He will sustain us either by *performance or provision.*

Another reason we refuse to move in an act of faith is because:

2. Our trust in God's plan is based on our own ability and resources to carry it out.

If we couldn't plan our way through it, we just weren't going to go through with it. But, of course, we wouldn't dare be so brazen or openly rebellious against God. No. What we do is just convince ourselves that God couldn't have asked us to move. This type of reasoning is completely fallible, and goes against the identity of God being omnipotent. This type of logic makes God just as the Greek gods and goddesses. In that polytheistic arrangement between gods and human, the gods' power is drawn from the people. If the people stop praying, the gods lose their strength. So, in turn, the gods send pestilence to garner the prayers of the people and retain their strength. God's power is completely operable outside of YOU. When you limit what He can do based solely on what you can do, you make Him dependent on you. You become His source, and thus, His God. You are not always going to get the details. Sometimes, God's insight comes in the way of instructions. Actually, more times than none, true faith in action will remove you from the detail and cause you to be in the place where you have to decide either to trust God with everything beyond a plan or not.

There are times when God calls us out and will afford us the privilege of knowing exactly what to do before we even begin to take the steps. This instruction requires obedience. The level of faith that is achieved here is the faith to believe. God says "here is what I will do, here is what will happen" and we, in faith, believe it to be so. But, beyond the faith to believe is the faith to act. This is what happens when God doesn't tell us the how, the what, or any of the relative details of His plan. All He says is "move". Now as an adult when you encounter this level of faith in life, you may find yourself in conflict with your adult responsibilities. What if God says "leave your job" as He did with me? It would be crazy for you not to question Him about the details and plan. This is your livelihood. This is your income. This is your obligation. If you are consulting others; most, if not all, will first ask you for the plan. They are considering the reality of the situation because well, that is what plans usually address: the realities. I am not telling you that you are wrong to have the questions, but I am telling you that sometimes, those questions aren't answered beforehand. I'm also not saying we should be irresponsible or reckless. Faith will often look risky to the natural eye. But risky isn't reckless. The bible teaches that we are not to tempt the Lord, so for us to put ourselves in situations unwise is not an opportunity to expect "faith" to work.

Most of us in this part of our lives have been through enough disappointments and failures that we know it to be wise to have developed our back-up systems. We have grown accustomed to having a plan A and, more often than not, a plan B and C ready to implement. But, ask yourself, are you truly trusting God if you have to know before you go? What about those of us who go but have our "just in case this doesn't work out" plan B all ready for when God's plan fails us. That sounds strange, doesn't it? The concept of God failing, when you verbalize it, is bizarre, strange even. He wouldn't fail us. He can't fail. We know this and we preach this; but, do we really live this? What is a 'plan B' but a cushion for the possibility that plan A won't work? You may not want to hear this, but the truth is every time we bring our own plan B along into the unknown plan of God carried out through an act of faith, it is an unspoken admission which says to Him "this is just in case you fail". Let that sink in.

Family, we all have been there. We are human, and socialized to evidence, to tangible, visible, careful proof. When you find yourself doubting, however, the answer isn't to make your own back-up plan by trying to secure your own footing. Rather, it is to pray and ask God to strengthen you in your area of unbelief. Carrying your back-up into the act of faith is believing God partially; like trusting Him, but with the side-eye. Listen carefully, there is no such thing as partial faith. You may have doubts, you may have fears, but faith requires all of you and nothing less.

Are you ready to lose your POWER? Remember, acts of faith don't require your help, just your obedience and will go against your flesh.

Time to READ
REFLECTION EVALUATION ADMISSION DECISION

R-eflection

What initial thoughts and/or emotions did you encounter while reading this chapter? Name and explore them in connection with this idea of control.

E-valuation

Have you ever been, or felt as though you were, made powerless in a situation? List the feelings attached to this reality. Have you ever been disappointed when you trusted someone else? List the feelings attached to this reality. Are there shared emotional responses on these two lists?

A-dmission

Lack of control often causes us to have to be open and vulnerable, which for many people, is scary. Are you someone who has to be in charge of the situation at all times? Why? What does being in-control provide you? Where does the need to be in control come from? Do you believe your need for control has anything to do with your vulnerability? Discuss. Have you healed from any instances wherein you were vulnerable and may have been hurt/disappointed therein? Or, have you simply moved on from hurt with a hardened and distrusting heart?

D-ecision

What things need to happen in your life (and within your control) and what action steps will you take towards those directives in order for you to trust again?

4- SEEING BEYOND *FLESH*

As I mentioned before, walking away from my job was extremely hard for a number of reasons. The biggest of those reasons was simply it made no sense at all for me to so. Consider this:

1. Prior to starting this job in April of 2014, I had not collected a check that reflected a full-time work schedule in nearly a year and a half.

2. I attempted, multiple times, to file for unemployment benefits in separate jurisdictions and was denied each time. Due to governing policies, my places of employment (which were non-profits) were not required to report employee wages. So for the three years I worked in those positions, no one had record of me working, even though the taxes I paid stated otherwise. And, when one chose to report them, I was deemed ineligible since I chose to leave my part time employment to complete my full-time education.

3. Due to the lack of income, struggle was not only inevitable, but it became a perpetual state. I was without the ability to provide for myself the most basic

of needs. There is almost nothing more disturbing for a man than being unable to provide. A man who is comfortable with his inability to or inactivity of providing is one who is dangerous. Not only will he actively seek opportunities to drain from others, but he will do so without care and, ultimately, create a life and identity built on the backs and efforts of everyone but himself. So, ladies, do beware. But, I digress. I borrowed from every source to which I was connected. My primary source, however, was my mother; she paid everything! Every bill, every utility, insurance, rent, gas…if I needed it, used it, or created it; she paid for it. (Shoutout to mothers, you guys are simply the best!)

I cannot explain how completely emasculating this was. When I finally moved out the house at the ripe age of 26, I had no intention of ever having to go back. Blame it on a healthy mixture of pride and, well, pride, but having already wrestled with the reality that I was behind in so many areas of my life (no career, no degree, no family, no love interest, etc.), going back to live with my parents would've been a dagger in my already low self-esteem. Moving out was all I had that represented any semblance of independence and self-sustainability. I was proving something to myself and, at this point, I needed to believe in me more than ever before. So, there I was, living every day in lack, believing less and less in my abilities, negotiating more and more with my identity, and questioning the accuracy of God's timing. Things had gotten so rough, that there was a period of time (about 10 months) where

I could do no grocery shopping. I mean, sure, some slight bread and milk here and there, yes; but my shelves and cabinets were never full.

Things were bad. I had everyone praying, mostly because I myself had grown tired of talking to God about the same stuff. You ever been there- in that place where your prayers sound more like cries of frustration? Where you get tired of being reminded of your problems so you just don't mention them? Or where you grow so weary of dealing with the same issue that even discussing it emotionally exhausting? My humble petitions to the Lord had (im)matured into impatient demands and temper tantrums. "Don't you see me!?", "Aren't you concerned about my plight?!", "How are you getting glory out of this?!" I was extremely frustrated with God and with life. It felt as though he had forgotten me and wasn't interesting in remembering. It seemed as if He had grown stale of our connection and stopped trying to reach me. I was confused and unsure if this place was the result of my own actions or if this was where I was supposed to be. Whatever it was or for whatever reason it came to be, I didn't like it. I didn't know what to do, so I stopped doing anything. I stopped applying for jobs after a while. I was sure I had sent my resume or filed an application with every company of which I could think. I applied to jobs for which I was extremely over-qualified, as well as jobs I had no chance of getting. At this point, I didn't care! I applied for jobs in every industry. I was open to every schedule...I was completely without preference. It had gotten so bad, that I put in job offers at places and for positions that I knew had NOTHING to do with God and were completely out of my character. I once submitted an application to be a bar back in a place where I would've never been comfortable without compromising. Yeah, I was desperate. But, even in all that, still nothing. No leads, no call backs, nothing. Then, out of the blue, something falls in my lap. Process went smoothly, and before I knew it, I had finally been offered a position that paid me extremely well, with benefits and some other perks I could enjoy. All this, and still I was being lead to walk away.

LEAVING MADE NO SENSE; not to me, at least. And, I knew if I couldn't understand it, surely no one else would. Here I was in a position where I was finally able to be fully self-sufficient after years of being dependent upon others for the basic needs of life; yet, I was about to quit my job. This couldn't have been God. The same God who heard and honored my cries for ample subsistence was now leading me back into a place of complete uncertainty…what logic would that be?

Hesitation to move in an act of faith usually exists because acts of faith prove to go against the assurances of the flesh. Think about the aspects of our humanity operating within us that bring a sense of security. There's this ever-present need to know things; for the sake of our security, of course. I mean, God did say "for lack of knowledge people perish" right? And then, of course, there's our understanding, which we just so happen to be able to justify with scripture. The word does say "in all thy getting, get understanding", right? In addition to those, there is logic and rationale, reasoning and justification; all of which are concepts born of our natural man that allow things to "make sense". Sociologists would say that we have all these innate cognitive functions in order to help us operationalize things. In other words, we have to make sense of things (in some acceptable way or another) so that we can put them into practice, or operate them. All of these human practices work within our intelligence to give us a sense of stability and allow us to feel and operate comfortably within the situations that come our way. The problem arises when we take into account the limitations of our own intelligence. We can only make as much sense of something as our capacity for reasoning allows, and when we are limited in that capacity, our sense of a thing is also limited.

Acts of faith, however, interrupt that security by forcing our dependence on God and His system. I believe this is what is depicted when the scripture says "for we walk by faith not by sight" (2 Corinthians 5:7). It's not that God expects us to walk around blindly with our eyes literally closed, but He does want us to move our assurance beyond the systems of our natural man upon which we have become so heavily reliant. Faith makes you depend on something that can't be measured or, at times, even understood. The processes don't always add up and, for many of us, it's a challenge to live life based upon a system in which our inherent humanity has so many questions. We are wired to want to know! It's so embedded in our nature that God used the wisest king that ever lived to speak on it.

Solomon teaches us in Proverbs 3:6 to "lean not to our own understanding, but rather acknowledge Him in all our ways and He would direct our paths". Here we find Solomon teaching the principle of living by faith. Faith works against every human operative and trait we have (our understanding) and the reason it is so hard to practice in completion is because being human is more natural. It's so natural, that trying to make sense out of things happens even without our permission. The human nature of our wondering and curiosity are instinctive. Of the two ways to live, sight (humanity based logic) and faith, the latter is the one that takes an intentional effort to put into practice. **Remember, our default nature is our humanity, not our faith**. Faith is divine. Hebrews tells us that faith comes from God, with Christ himself being the author. And because we are both human and divine, in that we exist in the likeness of God, we have a propensity and capacity for both faith and humanity. However, the truth is we are more comfortable and conditioned in our humanity than our faith because it is where we have been developed. So, we naturally rely on the socially developed human aspects more.

Think about children, for instance. A child isn't concerned about what sense something makes. Think about the things in which you believed as a child. Santa Claus, tooth fairies, monsters in the closet, etc. The thing about children is they are not conflicted with realities connected to logic or their sense of reality intelligence. At their young age, it is not as developed as it is in our adulthood! All they have is this sincere, unquestionable, innocent reliance upon mom and dad (or some trusting adult). Children demonstrate belief that doesn't waver or gives way to what makes sense. Maybe this is why Christ taught the disciples that the kingdom of God would only be received by coming in the manner of children (Matthew 18). This is how we were made to exist, with a faith that's childlike but not childish. We've allowed our human nature to break our dependence on and connection to

God. But, it's not all our fault, so don't feel too bad. This, like all our other issues, is ultimately a result of our progenitors and first parents, Adam and Eve.

In the beginning, we find beautiful interaction with God and man. Harmoniously perfect. However, this harmony was disrupted with one single act of man, with a consequence introduced in scripture by the statement "their eyes were opened" (Genesis 3:7). The word of God doesn't mention one thing about their sight (the awareness of their humanity) until after they disobeyed. It wasn't merely the sin that caused their eyes to be opened and their system of sight to operate over faith; it was the object of their disobedience, the fruit. The bible makes it clear that the tree that was forbidden to eat from was the tree of the *knowledge* of good and evil. It was this hunger for KNOWLEDGE over the instruction and dependence on God that betrayed Adam and Eve in their relationship with Him. And, just like our first parents, it is this same hunger and choice to depend on this human capacity that does the same to us in our relationship and harmony with God today. No, I am not saying that knowledge isn't useful or that it shouldn't be pursued. I am currently a student as I write this sentence; just finished my semester actually. But, human knowledge and intelligence can pose a threat to our faith. Paul said it this way:

> "**3**For we are the circumcision, who worship by the Spirit of God__b__ and glory in Christ Jesus and ***put no confidence in the flesh***— **4**though I myself have reason for confidence in the flesh also. If anyone else thinks he has reason for confidence in the flesh, I have more:

_5_circumcised on the eighth day, of the people of Israel, of the tribe of Benjamin, a Hebrew of Hebrews; as to the law, a Pharisee; _6_as to zeal, a persecutor of the church; as to righteousness under the law,_c_ blameless. _7_But whatever gain I had, I counted as loss for the sake of Christ. _8_Indeed**, I count everything as loss because of the surpassing worth of knowing Christ Jesus my Lord**. For his sake I have suffered the loss of all things and count them as rubbish, in order that I may gain Christ _9_and be found in **him, not having a righteousness of my own that comes from the law, but that which comes through faith in Christ, the righteousness from God that depends on faith**—"

If anyone had reason in which to be confident, it was Paul. But, even the well-educated, well-traveled, multi-lingual, zealous Paul understood that all of that, while commendable, had no place in the system of faith. Truth is, the longer we live, the more time and opportunity life has to build up our humanity causing us to practice it by default. But when we become too confident in and contingent upon the self-sufficiency of our sight, we compromise our ability to trust in God's sufficiency through faith, giving it no room to rule in our lives. *We walk by sight, not by faith.*

I know that it may be hard to hear or even accept, but it's true nevertheless. We have lived based on our system so long that we constrict and limit God by unconsciously forcing him to operate within that system, as well. Okay, maybe we don't make God operate by our system, but we do use it as the lens through which we view Him, His abilities, and His promises. Faith in God should not be based on the limited scope of our humanity. Paul told the church at Corinth "and my message and my preaching were not in persuasive words of wisdom, but in demonstration of the Spirit and of power, so that your faith would not rest on the wisdom of men, but on the power of God" (1 Cor. 2:4-5). We will fail ourselves every time if we attempt to understand God by using our own humanity as a standard. It could never make sense if left up to our logic. He's big and we are too small. He's perfect and we are too flawed. He's infinite, we are limited. He knows more than we can even know to imagine. We, even in our greatest heights and abilities, could never fully understand His mind; for His thoughts and His ways are much higher than our own. Could you imagine if God's actions were dictated solely by what you were capable of understanding? Where would your salvation be, then? A perfect and Holy God giving His son to die as a ransom for the transgressions of imperfect people makes no sense whatsoever.

Faith isn't based on our system of "sight". Rather, it works against that practiced humanity; a humanity which, through said practice, has been perfected. No, you aren't a perfect human but you are a perfected one. And in the same way that life causes us to become better at being humans (not necessarily better humans), we need something that pushes us to become better at faith.

The writer of Hebrews describes Christ as the author and PERFECTER of our faith, because this system that is foreign to us can only be forged by intentional efforts of development. For this reason, the things that God asks of us and says to us won't develop our humanity, but will challenge us to grow in the places where true faith is lacking. Look at it biblically, where do you find acts of faith that make sense or appease to our humanity? Should we look at Abraham? We know the story, senior citizen couple having a child. As a matter of fact, they would be great-grandparents, maybe even great, great-grandparents at their age these days. They were so old, Abraham laughed when God told him his barren wife would conceive. It didn't appeal to his logic. Nevertheless, it happens, and Isaac becomes the son of promise, through which the blessing of Abraham would be continued and fulfilled. Then what happens? God tells Abraham to sacrifice him.

See, family, it isn't our intelligence, our reason, or our logic that impresses God; it is our FAITH. Hebrews 11:6 states that "without faith, it is impossible to please Him". To use our definition, God takes pleasure in being invited to be involved in our lives and to do so with an influence drawn from His insight, instruction, and inspiration. The question thus becomes if God is only pleased by our faith, why do we expect him to appease our humanity? This is why the very aspect of you that makes and justifies your existence as a human being is made invalid by faith. This faith will allow you to meet a challenge in his instruction with a response by way of action, and it will all require you to move beyond YOU. Your intelligence, your reasoning, your logic all have to be defeated and removed from the place in which it is allowed to dictate your actions. *The things God will ask of you won't always make sense; but, they will make faith.*

Time to READ
REFLECTION EVALUATION ADMISSION DECISION

R-eflection

What initial thoughts and/or emotions did you encounter while reading this chapter? Name and explore them in connection with this idea of living based on your own humanity.

E-valuation

Have you ever felt lead to do something that didn't make any sense to your innate humanity? When do you feel the most secure? How have you practiced and perfected your humanity?

A-dmission

What is the hardest part about trusting without seeing? Have you ever felt let down by God, even if for a moment? What is/are the cause/s of your absence of faith? Have you felt betrayed by your own expectations? Examining those instances, what was the extent in which your own human agency added to the feelings your experienced?

D-ecision

What things need to happen in your life (and within your control) and what action steps will you take towards those directives in order for you to learn to live beyond your own sight?

5- SEEING BEYOND *DISCOMFORT*

- Listening to "Beautiful Things", Gungor

"Perfect" is one of the oft misinterpreted words in the bible. Reason being, there are so many definitions for this one word mentioned multiple times throughout scripture. God is perfect (without blemish, spot, or fault), and looks to perfect (make complete) us that we may be perfect (complete, mature, lacking nothing). See? Now there are those who think that we are to be perfect and without flaw, like God. Well, the word also lets us know that we won't be as He is until we see Him. However, while this flawlessness is impossible to achieve in our nature and immediate time, God does still expect us to be PERFECTED, or complete and mature, in areas that are underdeveloped.

As mentioned in the previous chapter, the development of faith is an intentional occurrence and it has to be due to the fact that we are so accustomed to the ways of our humanity. But, remember, the humanity in which we've grown accustomed is still of a fallen nature, not the one of our originally created state. If any of you are techies, then think of it like a smartphone. When you get a new phone, if you're anything like I am, you start installing things almost immediately. Games and apps and all sorts of other upgrades that make the phone "better" in your eyes. However, the manufacturer will always warn the customer that downloading these external programs and software on the device puts it at risk of improper operation. As a matter of fact, even as I type this, my 6-month old Galaxy S5 needs to be master reset because its speaker function hasn't worked in about two months. (I hate master resetting, that's why I've just dealt with the no sound. I should get around to it soon though). Look at us like those phones. We were made in a state of perfect operation, but downloaded some outside software and now are operating outside of maximal functioning. So, it's as if God is trying to get us back to the "default setting" if you would. We're in need of master reset; "the Master's reset" to be more exact. Getting back to living in and upon that system of faith must be of an intentional effort. And, truth be told, that's not always comfortable.

Now again, faith has to be perfected. Who better to do so than the one who is perfect in faith? (Jesus, the author and perfecter of our faith) The body is great illustration of what happens during the teaching phases of faith. I work out. I'm a fan of the gym. I actually really enjoy going. So, when we work out, we usually focus our efforts on a particular area. If you want results on your chest, you do chest exercises like a bench press or a fly. You don't do leg press or stair climbers. No, we use focused and intentional exercises for the area we need to be developed. Interestingly enough, whatever muscle you're building during weight training is actually more stressed as you work it out. Makes sense, though. In order for something to be developed, it has to be worked. That working usually puts a lot of stress and strain on that particular area. Now, just as with working out, the process of being perfected is never an easy or comfortable one; and, is usually filled with a bunch of stressing and straining as we, like our muscles, engage growth. James said it like this, "count it all joy when you find yourself in divers situations, knowing that the trying of your faith worketh patience, and let patience have her perfect work so that you may be complete, lacking nothing" (James 1:2-4). This scripture captures the message of this entire chapter. Even without trying, we are being ever-perfected in our humanity; so God has to counter that by perfecting us in our faith. The perfecting process is done through building patience which is brought about by TRIALS (Romans 5). At the end of a grueling workout, I'm sore because the process to grow my muscle was not comfortable for the muscle. What does that mean for you and me? Simple. *Faith can only be grown and developed by an exercised effort that stresses and stretches the faith which is already present.*

"But wait!", you say, and I already know what's next. Yes, the bible does in fact teach that faith comes by hearing the word of God. I'm in absolute agreement with this statement. But, while faith COMES by hearing the word of God, it only works when it's ENGAGED. Faith only works on us when we work it. It would be like going to the gym just to look at the machines. It's there but, by only looking, I am in no way benefitting from its existence. *The development of faith is a participatory process.* God challenges us with His word (faith coming) but we have to do something with what He gives (faith engaged). This is why James says:

22But be doers of the word, and not hearers only, deceiving yourselves. **23**For if anyone is a hearer of the word and not a doer, he is like a man who looks intently at his natural face in a mirror. **24**For he looks at himself and goes away and at once forgets what he was like. **25**But the one who looks into the perfect law, the law of liberty, and perseveres, **being no hearer who forgets but a doer who acts**, he will be blessed in his doing.

What James is saying here is that encountering the word of faith and not engaging in the act it prompts is the behavior of the man only focused on his natural self. And the flaw with being so focused on the capabilities of your natural self, in his opinion, is that you are always drawn back to you. The man looks intently upon himself, then leaves and forgets; which means what? What do you usually do when you forget what something looks like? Exactly! You, just like this man, turn back and look again. He looks, turns away, and forgets; only to have to go back, immediately, to look again. Sight-based living is SIGHT BASED. And, since it is limited to only what you can see, what we deem as possible is also limited to the actuality of what already is, not what can be. When we fail to engage faith, we trap ourselves in this cycle of sight-based living.

So it takes engaging in acts of faith to build faith and, just like that dreadful workout, it's rather uncomfortable. But it is discipline and Hebrews 12 puts it very clearly "No discipline is enjoyable while it is happening--it's painful! But afterward there will be a peaceful harvest of right living for those who are trained in this way" (Heb. 12:11). Discipline is training or instruction that molds and perfects one to a standard of behavior. God uses acts of faith to train and develop you in the system of faith-based living. It's not for nothing; it's literally designed to bring you back to a place of righteousness, where faith is the default. Now, I'm not saying you're living unholy or unrighteous, but it is important that we know it is neither our deeds nor our character that makes us righteous. We are considered righteous because of our faith. The bible says in Romans 4:5 that "And to the one who does not work but believes in him who justifies the ungodly, his faith is credited as righteousness" (NASB).

God is producing a harvest of faith by offering us the opportunity to engage in acts of faith. The more you are developed in faith, the more you begin to confidently live by its mode of operation. However, development here takes engaging in the training that comes with the acts of faith he puts before you. Enter circumstances.

Time to READ
REFLECTION EVALUATION ADMISSION DECISION

R-eflection

What initial thoughts and/or emotions did you encounter while reading this chapter? Name and explore them in connection with this idea of having to be disciplined in faith.

E-valuation

How would you rate yourself in the area of discipline? How do you promote and practice discipline in your life on a daily basis? How has being comfortable caused you to miss any opportunities or surrender chances for growth?

A-dmission

Development often comes through the crucible of challenge; in what ways are you consistently and actively being challenged to become your best self and what systems do you have in place that push you beyond your own comfort?

D-ecision

What things need to happen in your life (and within your control) and what action steps will you take towards those directives in order for you to learn to live beyond being comfortable?

6- SEEING BEYOND *CIRCUMSTANCES*

-Listening to "I Am", Jason Nelson

I come from a pretty close-knit family. We do a lot together. Many of us attend the same church. We live in neighboring communities. We have keys to each other's houses. Some of us even share friends. After my father passed away in March 2010, we decided to start hosting what we called "First Sundays", where we intentionally came together on the first Sunday of each month for dinner and fellowship. I say intentionally because, for us, family dinners happened (and happen) all the time without prior planning. Anyways, we would sit for hours after dinner on those Sunday evenings enjoying conversation, laughs, and of course watching our favorite family show Criminal Minds. Listen, my family LOVES some Criminal Minds. Let us tell it, we are pretty much just as good as the FBI's Behavioral Analysis Unit. From NYPD Blue and New York Undercover, to NCIS and CSI (Miami, of course); we are pretty much pros at catching criminals. Add in Law and Order (SVU) which gives us even further view into the actual courtrooms and we could seriously all vie for the next open District Attorney position.

Okay, maybe that was an exaggeration, but we did learn a lot from watching these shows. One of the terms that we became very familiar with was *Circumstantial Evidence*. According to legaldictionary.com, circumstantial evidence is "information and testimony presented by a party in a civil or criminal action that permit conclusions that indirectly establish the existence or nonexistence of a fact or event that the party seeks to prove." In layman's terms, circumstantial, or indirect, evidence allows one to draw a conclusion based on the looks of things. For instance, direct evidence would be if you made a claim that it rained based on the FACT that you looked out the window and literally saw the precipitation falling from the sky. Circumstantial evidence, however, would be you stating it rained because you saw the ground was wet, smelled the fresh scent of rain water in the air, or even heard the beating of the drops on the window. In other words, you drew a conclusion based solely on "the look of things". Hmmmm, I'll let that one sink in.

Here's what we are dealing with…faith brings us to a crossroads wherein two perspectives collide: the perspective of truth and the perspective of reality. And, no, these two are NOT always the same. Truth, as we understand it, is determined by the weight we put in the source from which it originates. It should be seen as that which exists in accordance with what has been evidenced, factualized and exact. It is objective and usually accepted without debate or argument, as it has been tested and proven over time. But, reality is often different. It is more personal, biased even. It is subjective, and the sum of one's particular experience and discourse. Reality speaks to what has become real and relevant to self. Right now in my life, I am facing the confrontation of these two opposing entities and, if you have no fact or proof to believe otherwise, you will accept anything as truth until it is tested.

My truth is not my reality, and has not been for some time now. My reality is very, well, real. I see it daily. I feel it daily. No job, no finances, and the slew of problems that arise from that. Reality can be defined as the sum of circumstances sensory present which has the ability to affect us directl. Reality is what has been currently made manifest. It is visible and for many of us, initially at least, defies the truth of our faith. However, in the midst of that reality, I hold on to a truth. Truth has nothing to do with what I see, but everything to do with what I've heard from God. So how do we navigate life in the pendulum of these two forces?

Here's what I want you to know, *you can't ignore reality.* Don't believe that you can or that you should, even. Ignoring reality, or doing as I did and trying to avoid the reality, only makes things worst. I refused to open bills, refused to take calls from collectors, refused to own my reality. Did you know that things don't go away simply because you refuse to acknowledge them? Ignorance doesn't negate existence. However, we can get peace regarding our realities if and when we give them to God. Depending on the perspective from which you view life will determine how you navigate and maneuver in the bouts of faith. If you live from a place of your truths instead of your reality, you will find yourself doing things that don't necessarily add up or fit the restrictions of that reality.

It was Wednesday, October 1ˢᵗ 2014 when I made the decision to submit my two weeks' notice. For months, I had been praying about it with hope of shaking the unsettling feeling; however, I could not escape the level of discomfort that burdened my spirit as it related to remaining on the job. I was miserable. I was certain I was hearing God because the unrest I was feeling internally was so uncomfortable. I was nervous, but knew I had to move even though I had no idea where. What I did know was that in spite of my uncertainty, not moving was not an option. I had learned through experiences before, both mine and others, the danger of remaining in places where God has released or required you to move from. Being there will cause a great discomfort in your spirit, but remaining there when called out will cause an ever greater displacement of your life.

So, I waited all day before putting in the notice with my supervisor. I was extremely apprehensive of the imminent conversation and what I felt would be a confrontation with her. I do not know what I thought was going to happen, as if she would hold me hostage or yell at me for leaving. But, I figured something would happen that I would not like. So at the very last minute of the workday, I walked into her office with folded resignation letter in hand and began the speech I had rehearsed. I may have gotten about five words out before the spirit of God instructed me to speak from the heart.

I thought I would owe an explanation for my decision. That I would be challenged and made to feel a certain way about the decision I had come to. Has an act of faith ever had you so worried about how others would take it that it held you hostage?

Have you rehearsed some made up excuse to justify to someone else? This is where I was, that was until God released me in the moment. I found myself moving away from the script I had prepared. I was not leaving due to some personal reason that I had to hide. I was leaving because I heard God tell me to move. Stop being ashamed of the decision you're making because of how someone else will see it. Furthermore, stop using others as the excuse for not doing what God has called you to do. People won't always understand the faith you walk out, but those people did not hear the Lords instruction to you…you DID!

Here's the difference that we find in the story of Peter walking on the water. Peter didn't have to try to convince others of what he heard because, we can assume, they heard the same thing. I mean, they were right there in the boat with him. They saw what he saw, they heard what he heard and, up to this point, they had experienced Christ in the same way Peter did. As a matter of fact, they had all just witnessed him feed 5000 men, plus women and children to fulness, plus leftovers, with what was barely enough for you or me. So, what made the others not move in faith as did Peter? Easy. It was their view of the circumstances. How you perceive anything will always influence what you reason from it and how you respond to it.

Faith should always take a superior stance. Keep these things in mind:

1. Faith doesn't wait for the circumstance to change.

When Peter goes over the side of the boat in Matthew 14:28-30, nothing about his circumstance had changed. There was still a storm on the sea, the winds were violent enough to shake a boat filled with a number of grown men, and the water was splashing and crashing and beating against the vessel enough that these men were fearful. Yet, Peter, at the command of Christ, steps out anyway. Take note that whether he would've stayed in the boat or not; he was still in a storm. Often times, we neglect to act in faith because we have taken refuge in "false shelter" and we fail to realize that it doesn't change the circumstance. If you're going to die in a storm, why not die in the storm trying to make your way to LIFE, or at least to the one who holds life in his hands. If you are going to be broke, why do so working that job you hate instead of doing so building the business in the field you love (per God's instruction). If you must exist in a circumstance ANYWAYS, why not exist there exercising FAITH!?

Check this out, though. Peter steps out the boat and starts to walk on the water. The bible says nothing about the properties of the water changing. It didn't freeze over and become ice. No fish came and held him up bearing his weight with each step. No, the water remained in a liquid state. It had to have been because the bible says that Peter saw the winds. You can't physically observe wind until it's affecting something you can see, like...you guessed it, water! Faith doesn't need my circumstance to change because *God doesn't require favorable conditions in order for His will to work*. As a matter of fact, the bible tells me that God specializes in the situations that, to man, seem impossible. When God calls you out, He is well aware of the current situation in which you're found. When we exercise a faith based in who God is and not our circumstances, we will change our prayers, realizing that things don't have to change, they just need to know their place in His will. Faith knows that the circumstance doesn't have to work WITH GOD, it just needs to work FOR GOD and FOR OUR GOOD!

2. Faith doesn't stop working in the midst of the circumstance.

Here is what I had to understand, faith is not one step. Nope, not at all. The act of faith is a series of steps that reflects and requires obedience and patience, as well as diligence in seeking God. Let's go back to Peter. The bible says that he steps out of the boat after being summoned by Christ' instruction in response to his request to walk on the water. However, Peter's faith wavers while walking, causing him to sink into the fell clutches of his circumstance. Christ admonishes Peter by saying "ye of little faith". Herein lies our issue. Peter gets out of the boat and continues to move forward.

He did not take one step and stand on the water, but he moved diligently-driven towards the voice of God. I believe that he was relying on what he had heard in his spiritual connection with Christ more than what he could see being as though the circumstances around him were not conducive for a conversation. It was a storm, pouring rain sharply piercing the sea. There were violent winds that caused the boat to rock. The bible says that he saw the waves, which means that they were crashing along the shores, alongside the boat, and against one another. It was not just a sight to see, but it was sound to hear. Yet, Peter did not stop moving in the way of instruction from God that was spoken to him.

When you make this move of faith, it's going to take some certainty in the area of your truth. What has God said about you? What has God said to you? The word of God has to be what you operate on and in, because the reality of your circumstances may just get louder and more prevalent before they get any better. You have got to hold on to your truth in spite of the circumstance that will inevitably come to defy it. But, be clear, before you can hold to truth, you first have to know it.

Just as Peter kept moving, initially, the same must be the case with us. Sometimes we think God calls us out and then stops talking. However, many times when we can't hear God, it isn't that he stopped speaking, but just the circumstance has just gotten too loud. Instead of it causing us to stop, lose progress, and ultimately sink beneath our issues; it should cause us to listen with more intent, to concentrate with more focus. It should motivate us not to quit or go back, but to ignore the distractions that usually get louder when we step out the boat in an effort to train our ear to hear his voice. Keep this in mind, it was not until Peter stopped moving forward in that directive of Christ's voice that he then started sinking. When you stop moving to accomplish the act of faith, it is then that your circumstances regain power over you. For as long as you are obedient in action to the call of faith, as well as diligent and determined in seeking God and loyal to your truth; your circumstances will not have power to overtake you during this walk.

Time to READ
<u>R</u>EFLECTION <u>E</u>VALUATION <u>A</u>DMISSION <u>D</u>ECISION

R-eflection

What initial thoughts and/or emotions did you encounter while reading this chapter? Name and explore them in connection with this idea of having faith despite the circumstances.

E-valuation

Explore this concept of reality versus truth? How do you find this present in your life? Make a list of your truths (What God says about you). What circumstances in your present reality oppose those truths? How do you navigate the conflict? Have you ever been held hostage to a situation by the opinions, perceived reactions of others?

A-dmission

Many times, we wrongly believe that faith a one-step act when it is more often a process. Have you made this mistake in the past? Discuss. What boat is God calling you out of? Circumstances can sometimes be louder than the connection with God we have. Which is stronger for you and why?

D-ecision

What things need to happen in your life (and within your control) and what action steps will you take towards those directives in order for you to learn to live beyond being comfortable?

7- SEEING BEYOND *FAMILIARITY*

One of the hardest things I found in this entire lesson in faith was the intensity of its requirements. I suppose when one hears that all you need is faith the size of a mustard seed, it doesn't truly give the impression that much would be imposed or demanded. I mean really, how much can something so small really ask of you? But faith, even in its mustard seed state, carries a very large obligation. It kind of reminds me of children, newborns to be more specific. Little bundles of joy, they are both small and innocent, yet they come with such a great need from those in whose care they are entrusted. Then, it hit me. It isn't the size of faith that matters (mustard seed); it's the cause and, essentially, the consequence of faith that matters. The word of God teaches that to whom much is given, much would be required (Luke 12:48); and no truer statement can be said of faith. Faith is MUCH GIVEN. Think about what God gave us when he offered us the gift of faith.

1. **It is through faith that we have access to salvation in Christ Jesus and brought into harmony with God. (1 Peter 1:9)**

2. **It is with the tool and exercising of faith that we are able to please God. (Hebrews 11:6)**

3. **It is by faith that we are able to ask and receive the blessings of God. (Matthew 21:22)**

4. **It is by faith that we are counted as righteous in the sight of God. (Romans 4:11)**

5. **It is because of faith, acting as a shield, that we can extinguish the fiery darts that come from the enemies of God.**

6. **It is thanks to faith being authored and perfected in us that we are able to become the children of God .**

Faith is the agent, the transit, and the characteristic that moves us from our fallen state to a new place; and that new place is situated in the presence of God himself. Faith both propels us into and prepares us for the direction of God.

For the costs and benefits of faith, even a little demands a LOT of YOU! It takes humility and relinquished control. It takes patience and trust in systems in which we aren't used to operating. It takes resiliency and persistence; courage and resolve. It takes the ability to endure frustration and, at times, walk alone. However, the initial component of faith, starts with VISION. Understand this: faith cannot begin to matriculate or manifest without vision.

Be careful not to confuse vision for sight. We have already covered the conflicts that sight and sight-based living creates for our faith. Vision is the ability to see beyond what is and has been. Vision is directly connected to faith because, like faith, it moves pass the obvious limits of sight and extends into the realm of what is not or has not yet been made visible or manifest. People who live by faith HAVE to be visionaries. Faith is the HOW to the vision's WHAT. It is the means by which the vision is cast, received, and made plain; and, you cannot have ONE without the OTHER.

Living blindfolded means that I wholly embrace the idea of walking by faith and not sight. See, the issue with sight is that it keeps everything familiar and, while I enjoy some familiarity in life, it can become a hazard and a hindrance in the matters of faith. The truth is, sight gets us used to how things are in their current and present state. The more we see the same things, the more we become socialized to the conditions of that reality. The more we become conditioned, the more we become comfortable with how things are. This ultimately leads to a decreased expectation of anything different than we have accepted as the norm. Situations, circumstances, emotional and physical places in life…without VISION, we are left entrapped and imprisoned to the stations of SIGHT's limitations.

When we become conditioned to the limitations of our sight, we are restricted from the expectations of our faith. As we settle in this position of restriction, we reflect it in our attitudes, behavior, and language. We begin to say things like "I could never see myself…" or "I don't think I could…". We make excuses that keep us in the familiar place like "I'm too old to…" or "with my schedule, I just can't find the time to…" These declarations are reflections of our limited ability to see beyond where we are and what is present and are nothing more than a sign of fear; because we don't know what life outside of the familiar looks like and the thought of it is scary. From there, it's a domino effect in our lives. We only desire the familiar and can only embrace it. Beyond that, we only expose ourselves to the familiar and, subsequently, can only expect it. Many times, we don't see God do anything new in our lives or within our circumstances or even within us not because He's satisfied with where we are, but because we've grown too settled in this place. When we don't give God room for anything new, we are quietly telling Him "nothing else, God. I'm good with the familiar life".

If you want God to do something NEW, you have to start seeing and feeding the expectation of new. I think the bible says it this way "be ye transformed by the renewing of your mind" (Romans 12). Cultivate that attitude of faith in your life by exposing yourself to the stations and status that you're looking to attain. If you don't have vision, start spending time around people who do. Change your culture of familiarity to foster a new mind of faith. Don't be afraid of being open to God's unfamiliar, because He wants to introduce you to more of himself. Believe it or not, you have only seen but a mere fraction of who God is and what He can do in your life. God makes more of himself available for you as you grow in faith. Be careful of becoming satisfied, but rather use your experiences with God to fuel the hunger for more of him. You can't get the MORE of God when you expect NOTHING. Peter displayed this in his 'walk on the water' experience.

In Matthew 14, the disciples found themselves in a storm, at sea, on a boat, at night without Jesus. They are afraid and when they finally see Jesus, Peter makes a request of Him, "Bid me to come to you". But, why that request? Consider the fact that just a few chapters prior, the disciples were in a very familiar situation; in a storm, at sea, on a boat without Jesus (he was sleeping). That time, though, they wake him and, after criticizing their low level of faith, He speaks peace to the storm winds and they obey. So, fast forward a few chapters and the same situation comes a little later and Peter, instead of asking what he has already experienced God do in calming the storm, asks God for something new. God, I know you can speak to this storm and make it obey. I've seen you do it; therefore, it's fact. But where I have fact of who you are, I want more. So, I'm stretching in faith and asking you to do what I haven't seen you do just yet. **That, my friend, is faith.**

Stop settling for the same old stuff. God has shown you He can do level-A work, now trust him to go to the next level. Hasn't He proven himself trustworthy? Isn't He worth the certainty of what your sight says is risky? Sure, you can stay in the boat while He calms the seas again, but faith is about growing you as you are exposed to more of him. Faith says 'do something in me, give me the strength, the power, the time, the will, the mind…grow me to a place where I can handle the storm this time'. Peter would've never experienced the power of walking on water if it weren't for his progression of faith which was willing to ask God for more. I dare you to be like Peter and give God the opportunity to blow your mind with more of who He is.

As I'm writing this, I'm being both convicted and encouraged. For the last few weeks, I've resorted back to the same prayer (and frustrating demanding) of God that I had employed just a few years ago when the situation looked just like this. "God, I just need a job, anything to have some money coming in to the house." But, where will that put me in another six months? Same circumstance as past times, same prayer will most certainly lead me right back to the same outcome-frustrated in a job that I don't really want. It just donned on me that I need to change my prayers; and maybe you do, too. **Are your prayers a reflection of your frustration or your expectation?** I must have faith to ask God for the more, in line with the vision, giving Him room to do what I haven't seen but undoubtedly believe that He is able to do.

Remember, God is moved by your faith; it pleases him. But when your thinking has removed the possibility of something more becoming of that situation or that circumstance or that condition, you stop LOOKING for God to do anything more. And here is the things, God wants to do for you! Hebrews 11:6 states that God rewards those who diligently seek him. A derivative of Greek word rewards used in this context translates to meaning to pay for services; to give back, to re-pay, perform, restore, recompense, render, deliver again, give again. Seeking God in its original context means to require or demand. God is saying that He responds to those who are actively expecting Him to do more. When you stop expecting God, you close the door to His being a 'rewarder'.

Time to READ
<u>R</u>EFLECTION <u>E</u>VALUATION <u>A</u>DMISSION <u>D</u>ECISION

R-eflection

What initial thoughts and/or emotions did you encounter while reading this chapter? Name and explore them in connection with this idea of having faith beyond what's familiar.

E-valuation

Take a minute to write out the vision for your life (present and future). Is faith required to achieve the vision or is it all familiar? Have you noticed any shift in your attitude about faith over the last year? Five years? If so, explain the changes and when/why they happened. God can't move mountains if we keep him in a box. Are you prayers reflective of God's ability or not? In what ways are you disrupting the familiar in an effort to feed and grow your faith?

A-dmission

Are you expecting the familiar when it comes to God moving in your life or do you push the envelope by stretching your faith? Would God be pleased with your faith? Why or why not?

D-ecision

What things need to happen in your life (and within your control) and what action steps will you take towards those directives in order for you to learn to live beyond the familiar places?

8- SEEING BEYOND *PRIDE*

I wrestled for a while with the content and direction of this chapter. It had been very hard for me to come to reality and accept the truth of its teaching. This entire process- leaving the job, trusting God through it- was not the first act of faith that I had ever taken, but it was by far one of the most defining. What I mean is that so much clarity came to me in this process and helped me to understand so more about myself. But, the process of being defined, or redefined to be more accurate, is scary; especially for us who have our OWN MINDS, OWN AGENDAS, and who live in a society that encourages us to find our OWN WAY. We live life under this safety blanket we have woven together with thoughts and ideas of who we think we are. Then, in a moment, all of what we "knew" is pulled back and we are exposed as imposters.

There's an old adage that speaks of this truth. It says, "when people show you who they are, believe them." Well, I've learned that the same is true of God, even more so. When God shows you who YOU are, you should definitely believe Him. The un/fortunate thing about living by faith is that you are completely exposed to the developmental system of God; which, in order to be effective, must include evaluations. God, like the doctor, is not evaluating you wearing all your "stuff". The process and work of faith developing within you will automatically prompt for self-evaluation which measures in accordance to the standard of the system and its manager. In other words, where there is development, there must be evaluation; and, where there is evaluation, there must be a standard.

Needless to say, this process gave me some unwelcomed evaluation. I was twenty-nine and I had gotten very used to my ways, actions and thoughts; and to be honest, I wasn't interested in changing them. The problem was one of my "ways" included frequent failures to act in faith. See, God and I had been here before. I had been given prior and plenty instructions to DO; I just did NOT. He gave me ample opportunities to try; but, I did NOT. This time was different and with it came evaluation which showed me that what I thought was a simple issue of faith was, in actuality, something much deeper. Enter PRIDE and INSECURITY.

I never thought of myself as prideful. I mean, sure, I took pride in the works I did, the people I knew and connections that I had; but, *prideful*, nah. I thought of myself as quite the opposite. I thought of myself as quite humble, even though one who is would probably never boast of it. Besides, all the years of self-esteem struggles and self-image battles didn't exactly foster within me a sense of positive self-pride. But, leave it to God to show me who I was in a much different light. Now, I wasn't going around gloating or celebrating myself above others; and I didn't parade around as though I was full of myself. These were the demonstrations of pride as I understood it to be defined. However, I soon realized that that there was more to it than that. I find that with God, it's usually more to it than that, which is why we have to go to Him as a standard on these kinds of things. Man and God see differently, and so we define differently, and thus there's a different standard of measurement and evaluation. So, while we could be meeting the standard of man, we could be falling far beneath the standard of God. Either ways, God told me that pride was more than this over-confident opinion in one's self. I just assumed it was this attitude of "I" being the focus of my own attention that made God hate it. But, is God really that vain? Is it only the attitude of self-exaltation in itself that makes God upset? I mean, He's God, and He knows that; why would He be intimidated by your false sense of "self". No, my friends, it's more than that.

The reason God hates the position of pride is because it prevents growth. Pride exalts us beyond our actual stations into a dangerous place where we are unprepared to exist successfully. It then moves us into a space where we are unable to be taught or corrected. When we take the stance of being above the teaching and reproach of God, we become enemies of God. In his letter to the church at Ephesus, Paul writes "Therefore I, a prisoner for serving the Lord, beg you to lead a life worthy of your calling, for you have been called by God. Always be humble and gentle" (4:1-2). Paul immediately connects our lives to our calling, or purpose; and our calling to our character. Pride will interrupt the flow of this consistency. He further reminds us of the station of God in our lives by saying that "There is one Lord, one faith, one baptism, ⁶ one God and Father of all, who is over all, in all, and living through all" (4: 5-6). From this God, Paul says that we all have been given gifts through Christ and:

> "[12] Their responsibility is to equip God's people to do his work and build up the church, the body of Christ. [13] This will continue until we all come to such unity in our faith and knowledge of God's Son that we will be mature in the Lord, measuring up to the full and complete standard of Christ. [14] Then we will no longer be immature like children. We won't be tossed and blown about by every wind of new teaching. We will not be influenced when people try to trick us with lies so clever they sound like the truth. [15] Instead, we will speak the truth in love, growing in every way more and more like Christ, who is the head of his body, the church. [16] He makes the whole body fit together perfectly. As each part does its own special work, it helps the other parts grow, so that the whole body is healthy and growing and full of love."

So, Paul lays it out for us. It starts with a mind of humility that is able to recognize that God is over all, including oneself. From there, this constant recognition allows me to move to where I'm able to appreciate life as an opportune gift of God, seeing Christ as my head and example, and live humbly with a purpose to serve FOR him. However, when we are unteachable and uncorrectable, we move out of this place. When we fail to live with a mindset of humility and adopt an attitude of pride, we also fail to see God as "over all". Whenever we are unteachable and above God's discipline; we dethrone Christ as our head and enthrone ourselves as lord..

When we move from the place of humility, we render our gifts ineffective in Gods sight. Your actions can move God's position from "for you" to "against you"…and it's all a matter of pride. Pride is one of the few things the bible says God hates. Furthermore, it's the one things that prevents us from receiving the grace of God and, according to scripture, causes God to resist us (James 4:6). Resist, or rage against; oppose. God opposes the proud. Did you hear that. God opposes THE PROUD; not just the PRIDE, but those who are themselves proud. With this stance from God, moving AGAINST US, what true progress can we make in the things that pertain to Him? Consider your personal faith. Do you really want to be taking a step out of the boat when God is against you? You're going to need the grace of God on your side as you maneuver through this faith walk. And furthermore, in the matter of corporate kingdom culture, pride hinders the movement of the body. If we are prideful, we can't be fully equipped for the work of ministry. If we are not equipped (by God) to do the work, then either the work won't get done or the work will be laid on fewer workers than should be. Either ways, if the work itself is prohibited, then it restricts the edifying of the body. If the body remains malnourished, then we fail to reach the full stature of Christ. In other words, we as a church will exist beneath where God has called us to stand in the world. Sound familiar? If the body remains in that state, then we remain as children, being deceived and tossed by every fad, doctrine, and false truth that comes forth. If this happens, how will the body ever be healthy, growing, and full of love?

God hates pride because it prevents the progress of maturation, thus stifles the power and potential of the body of Christ as his representation in the Earth. If God has no representation, then love can have no manifestation. That's just the surface, though. If we look even deeper, we see that at its core pride prevents our becoming better by also prompting us to embrace a position where we indirectly protect the parts of us that are underdeveloped and promote the places where we have established pretentious security. It is here where we breed and feed insecurities. Whenever we hide behind these places, we refuse God the right to deal with us in those places where we truly need to be built.

Time to READ
REFLECTION EVALUATION ADMISSION DECISION

R-eflection

What initial thoughts and/or emotions did you encounter while reading this chapter? Name and explore them in connection with this idea of overcoming your pride.

E-valuation

In what places in your life are you exhibiting or living in pride? Is there anywhere you are unteachable, closed-minded, or, otherwise, against growing?

A-dmission

How have you fostered a mindset of pride in your life? Think about some places where progress has stalled in your life, can you find evidence of your pride there? What ways/measures have you taken to ensure you remain teachable and humble?

D-ecision

What things need to happen in your life (and within your control) and what action steps will you take towards those directives in order for you to learn to live beyond being prideful?

9- SEEING BEYOND *INSECURITIES*

Listening to "Worn", Big Daddy Weave

It's impossible to discuss pride without discussing the issue of insecurities. The two often go hand in hand; whether people realize it or not is a separate discussion. Everyone knows the story of Cain and Abel, right? Cain, the first born son of Adam and Eve, was a tiller of the land (a gardener) like his dad. The younger brother, Abel, was a shepherd of the flocks. They both were given this awesome opportunity to bring an offering to God, an opportunity that isn't mentioned as having been required in the bible. Cain brings of his harvest and Abel brings the first of his flocks. The bible makes it clear that God favored Abel's offering over Cain's, and thus accepted it. But, why? The bible suggests an answer to this in Hebrews 11. It says that Abel's offering was given in 'faith'. As a result of this treatment, Cain was angry. As a matter of fact, the bible states he was wroth. Here we find the first instance of insecurity in the bible. The word wroth means to set ablaze and to *fret self*. The actions of Abel provoked Cain to become not merely angry, but also worried within himself. Insecurities are nothing more than signs that we are uncertain of something pertaining to our inner-selves. ***Whenever you are intimidated by something on the outside, it is a sign that you are insecure about something on the inside.***

Here's what I did. I was so insecure about the God-given gifts within me that had gone undeveloped, that I couldn't celebrate or even honor anyone who resembled what I wanted to do, how I wanted to do it, or what I felt I was called to do. I wrote a song, but it went nowhere. Someone else writes a song and becomes a local and regionally recognized artist. I preached, poured my heart and soul into the study and delivery of the word of God, and no door opens. Someone else, younger, and less experienced does the same and is being invited to sit on panels and offered speaking engagements around the country. Or how about I start a business and it stalls after the first year. Someone else does the same thing, and it becomes an enterprise almost instantly. Now, you may say this was jealousy, and that's probably what it became but it started somewhere else. See jealousy creates resentment towards some other person, but insecurity creates and deepens resentment against oneself. So, I was threatened and mad, hurt and dejected, all at the same time. I felt like Cain, as God refused my offering and accepted someone else's over and over. The things in which I offered open celebration were also the cause of my private frustrations as they, through their earned successes, undermined my confidence and reinforced the reasons behind my insecurities.

Our insecurities cause us to separate ourselves and become paranoid with a mind of extreme competition and suspicion of threat. This kind of destructive mindset leads us to a place of stalled progress. Cain, or even myself, could've used the great things taking place in the lives of others as INSPIRATION to do better. However, insecurity does the opposite and instead of being inspired, we are insulted. The thing about insecurities is that when they are rooted and fed, they grow defensively in their offense. So instead of causing us to focus on building the places that are seen as deficient, they lead to us to either steal, kill, or destroy that which we see as the threat altogether. Whose mode of operation does that sound like? Cain's insecurities about his offering caused him to kill his brother instead of simply presenting a better offering. Like Cain, insecurities cause us to shift our attentions. So, instead of our focus being on presenting our best to God with what He's given us, we become intimidated by the people around us who are doing right with what God gave them. Insecurities counter inspiration and lead us to a place where we start to become more threatened by the God in others than we are trusting of the God in ourselves. By keeping our eyes and focus on the wrong thing; we will feed the wrong attitudes and producing the wrong actions. So, while inspiration can be of God, insecurity is not. Think about it, how is God ever threatened by Himself? If it were at all possible, the trinity wouldn't be able to work. There would be consistent and constant competition and no cooperation between its three parts. No! It is not of God, for He cannot stand divided against Himself (Matthew 12:25). If God moving in someone else puts unease within you, then you must ask the question: are you sure of the god in you? The source of insecurity I find stems from one of two places: lack of development or lack of truth.

Insecurity is nothing more than a great lack of confidence. That confidence, or lack thereof, either comes from the fact that something hasn't received the adequate development it needs to stand a chance or from a lie that we accepted as truth. When we use prideful antics to shield our insecurities, we prevent God from developing them, keeping us insecure. And, as long as we choose to believe the lie over the truth, we will never trust or prove the insecurity to be false. Whatever the cause or source, insecurities negate faith.

Insecurities give the holder a false perception that makes everything seem so much worse than it is in reality. Additionally, they make everything seem personal because they are so deeply rooted and we have for so long accepted them as part of who we are. So, every time someone else had success in places that I knew I had abilities, I took it as if God himself was teasing and taunting me. I felt like I was being bullied or picked on, as though I were the weird kid who sat by himself at lunch that all the other kids talked about and at whom they poked fun. How could I have faith in a God that disapproved of me? How could I have faith in a God who wasn't moved by me? How could I have faith in a God who slighted me; a God who chose others over me, time and time again? Do you know how it feels to be picked last for the team every time? That's what it felt like, except it was as if the game started and ended, and I still remained unselected. Insecurities turn us against the ones who love us the most, and cause us to become dependent upon the things that destroy us the worst. It's hard to pray to a God you don't trust. Even harder to worship a God you don't respect. Insecurities make us doubt God's love, denying the opportunity to prove it and, in turn, refusing to give him our own. Does this sound familiar?

Insecurity hosts very sensitive targets. Naturally, we don't expose the more sensitive things to danger or situations we feel are more high-risk. We put up more defenses for places that are more delicate than others. For instance, I've struggled with self-image for years, maybe even my entire life. I admittedly have a large forehead which I hate and it really causes me frustration and anxiety. Some days are better than others, as with anything; but for the most part I never forget that it's there. So, when my eight-year-old nephew says something about my head, I get offended and defensive. My sensitive area of insecurity has been exposed and, in my mind, perceived as an attack, So, my first and automatic response is to protect and defend at all costs. What that ends up looking like is a kid, who loves me undoubtedly and who doesn't know (or even care) anything about the issues I have within myself, making a light joke with no mal-intent and leads to my self-justifying and becoming aggressive without even trying. This is the power or control of insecurity. It causes us to throw up fences and defenses from everything and everyone without our conscious effort to do so. When we persist in these false and unsafe misperceptions of self, we barricade ourselves in a shield that we believe serves to protect the sensitive places from further damage. However, realistically this shield only further separates us from the one who can heal the causes of those wounds. Insecurity retards the very mind and attitude of faith that we need to develop the will to conquer and defeat it. This self-imposed protection is, in reality, a self-imposed destruction.

Now what? What do we do to defeat insecurity in order to move forward in faith? Let me say this, we won't ever be perfect until we see him for ourselves, so there will always be some part of us that needs further development. So, the first step to conquering the insecurity that is rooted in under-developed areas of our lives has to be:

1. To admit you have an issue/area of insecurity present.

John 8:32- You shall know the truth and the truth shall make you free. Admission is usually the first step of any process of deliverance and that's because it is necessary in order for any of the steps that follow to be effective. If you're in a burning building and you want to be rescued, you will most definitely need the assistance of the fire rescue team. However, before they can get there to assist you or instruct you in the way to safety, you've got to give them the location of where you are. When we refuse to admit where we are, how can ever truly expect to be freed from where we are? We can't. Such expectation is unfairly projected when the acceptance of our issue is continually rejected.

Keep this in mind- God already knows where you are and what you're dealing with. This admission is not for Him; it's for you. See, you can't heal what you first don't allow yourself to feel. By feel, I'm talking about more than just the physical effects, but to allow yourself to accept your truth. Denial perpetuates denial. The longer someone denies the truth of their condition, the longer they deny themselves freedom from that condition. In the first chapter of the book of Haggai, the people of God, after returning back to their land from exile, had allowed God's temple to sit unfinished for quite some time. The word of the Lord comes to them and says, "you people say the time is not come the time that the Lord's house should be built." These, the people of God, have denied the time and priority of rebuilding to dwell and focus on their own houses. Furthermore, their denial of the time and condition denied them the opportunity to flourish as God had intended. The prophet Haggai went on the say "...Consider your ways! You have sown much, and bring in little; You eat, but do not have enough; You drink, but you are not filled with drink; You clothe yourselves, but no one is warm; And he who earns wages, Earns wages to put into a bag with holes....You looked for much, but indeed it came to little; and when you brought it home, I blew it away." **(Haggai 1: 2-9).**

While denial is convenient, it's both counter-productive and dangerous to anyone who chooses to engage it as a practice. The truth is admission is uncomfortable because it moves from the false reality wherein we've allowed ourselves to exist and brings with it the added responsibility of taking some action. Usually, that action is inconvenient to our station and disruptive to the condition in which we've grown comfortable. However, if we are committed to growing in our faith, then that means we must be committed to being developed beyond where we've been. The next step in conquering insecurity, then, is:

2. To acknowledge the source or cause of the wounded/underdeveloped place (insecurity).

If admission is the first step in this process, then acknowledgement has to follow as second. Some of us are insecure because of wounds that we have allowed to go untreated for years. We say "time heals all wounds" but that's not completely true. Time only heals the wounds that have first been properly treated. Without proper treatment first, time will turn a simple wound into a life-threatening infection. With proper acknowledgement comes the task of figuring out not just what the issue is, but WHY the issue is. Should we fail to acknowledge the wounds, the places and sources of our insecurity, we will undoubtedly and continuously feel the effects of our neglect in our daily lives.

Let's say you wake up one morning with a horrible rash on your face. Naturally, you would immediately try and find out what produced it. Same with our insecurities, they each come with visible signs and symptoms of deeper issues that we must search to understand in order to rid ourselves of the visible outbreak. It's not enough and of no benefit to know what my issues are (symptoms) if I am not about to determine and cure the cause? The problem that many of us face in failing to see progress that endures is that we are treating the symptom and not the cause.

Let's go back to the rash example. If you wake up every morning with a rash on your face and you treat the rash with topical cream, just to go back to sleep and wake up the next day with the same rash, how much progress have you made? How long do you keep only treating the rash? At some point, instead of solely dealing with the symptom, you decide to investigate further and find out that you're allergic to the material of the new pillow covering you bought or the new detergent used to wash it. The point I'm making here is that in order to fully and more permanently resolve the issues that you see in your behavior, your temperament, your disposition; you have to first uncover the sources that may not be so evident. This is why David asked God to create in him a clean heart, because he knew all his issues started there. ***Proverbs 4:23-Keep your heart with all diligence, for out of it spring the issues of life.***

Once we have acknowledged the courses of our insecurities, our final step is:

3. **To allow God to heal or build the places of insecurity within us**.

In theory, this is simple. In practice, however, not so much. Many people have become so used to protecting the insecure places within themselves that the thought of exposing them or becoming vulnerable again is downright frightening. It's almost like when you had a really bad scrape and your grandmother had to put some alcohol on it to clean it up so it healed without possible infection. We knew we were hurting, but the idea of the burn from the alcohol always made us hesitant to give that wound proper treatment. At least this is how it was with me. In order to develop the underdeveloped places, we must trust the working process of God enough to give our deepest hurts, our scars, our wounds, our fears-all of our insecure places- over to Him. This process will call for patience which, when allowed, completes and matures us. And the issue with patience is it's brought about by trials. The word patience itself as used in the scripture even means tribulation, and the bible declares in Hebrews chapter ten that there is a need for patience. Like James said, we must let patience have her perfect work, for if Romans 5 is true, then we take glory in this process "knowing that tribulation worketh patience; And patience, experience; and experience, hope:" (5: 3-5). And what is hope but that which our faith reflects. Where there is no hope, there is no faith.

It won't be comfortable, and it may very well hurt or sting a little. However, we must remember that we are not alone in this. "Therefore we also, since we are surrounded by so great a cloud witnesses, let us lay aside every weight and the sin which so easily ensnares us, and let us run with endurance the range that is set before us, looking unto Jesus, the author and finisher of our faith, who for the joy that was set before Him endured the cross, despising the shame, and has sat down at the right hand of the throne of God" (Hebrews 12:1-2).

Time to READ
REFLECTION EVALUATION ADMISSION DECISION

R-eflection

What initial thoughts and/or emotions did you encounter while reading this chapter? Name and explore them in connection with this concept of insecurities affecting your daily faith.

E-valuation

Where are you (or have you been) worried within yourself? Where are you underdeveloped or otherwise over-guarded? Where/who do your insecurities come from? How have your insecurities shown up in your life (relationships, engagements, opportunities)?

A-dmission

Do you feel (or have you ever felt) slighted by the success of others? Explore and discuss these feelings? Where do you think they came from and why? What lies have you believed about yourself? Have you ever felt as though God was taunting or insulting you? How did that impact your relationship with Him? When celebrating others, do you ever feel the need to compare? Explain.

D-ecision

What things need to happen in your life (and within your control) and what action steps will you take towards those directives in order for you to learn to live beyond your insecure places?

10- SEEING BEYOND *SUPPORT*

"Forever Reign" by One Sonic Society

One of the most defining lessons in the process of acting out faith is the one of support. Let's be clear, we human folk are relational creature, and many times we make decisions with others in mind. I'd even venture to say that decisions are often influenced by the crowds. Crowds play a huge role in life, sometimes to our detriment. If they can be a reason why we choose to do one thing, they can be the same reason why we choose NOT to do another. CUE FAITH.

It was late February 2015 at this point when I received the revelation of this lesson in my life and process of faith. I told you that I had all this planned out before I even jumped out the boat. So, I was in the second semester of the year, which meant a refund check was on the way. This was necessary for my sanity as well as my security, as it would be the source of money for the necessities (rent, groceries, bills, gas, etc.) The semester started in early February, and the refunds were to be issued right around the middle of the month. So, I made all my financial arrangements around the expected date of disbursement. When mid-month came around I was excited and eager. I checked my account each day waiting for the funds to arrive. A week of checking, and nothing.

Two weeks, and nothing. So, I called and turned out the disbursement date was pushed back. Of course it was pushed back. I was heated, and beyond frustrated. I had been waiting since the beginning of the academic year and was being told I would now have to wait even longer. In my frustration, I vented to a friend. Now, I'm not sure what it was about the moment that inspired my friend to share their feelings but whatever it was, I was completely unprepared for what was coming. The friend went on to tell me, in so many words, how I made the wrong decision in leaving my job. They explained to me how it wasn't a wise decision on my part and how I should never make a choice like that again. They lectured me on my responsibilities and how I couldn't afford to be without a job because of said responsibilities. In short, they told me how they felt about my decision to act out obedience in faith. And I was floored.

It was definitely hard to decide to get out of the boat, but it had become so much harder when I realized that the support I thought I had, was merely a façade. This was probably the lowest of my moments in this experience up to that point. Think about it. Support helps hold you, it gives you an added assurance and confidence where there's doubt. To lose it or to have the perception of it changed so drastically was devastating, to say the least. I stopped. I stopped believing, I stopped moving. Just as with Peter, when he stopped moving along the water, I sank. I felt alone. With my support gone, the doubt came rushing back. If one person felt this way and just quietly sat back, how many other "silent naysayers" did I have. It made me question everybody who was in my corner. Maybe they were waiting for me to have this moment. To admit I was wrong in hearing God and in leaving the job. And, maybe I WAS wrong. Maybe I missed God completely on this one. Despite my prayer and fasting before making the decision, maybe I still missed God all the way. Did I allow the frustration of life to make me move and then say it was the leading of God? If I were that wrong about that, subconsciously, how could I trust my ability to hear God about anything at this point?

I was still frustrated and confused and doubting more, but I still needed answers about this money. At this point, I was about three months behind on rent, had no food in the house, insurance was nearing lapse, and bills were long overdue. I walked into the office that deals with the money disbursement (enrollment) and spoke with the VP of Enrollment, who told me that the dates had been pushed back for enrollment purposes and that the state would be disbursing the money somewhere around the end of the week. That meant that best case scenario I could expect money maybe the next week. That was a Tuesday. Two days later, on Thursday, for whatever reason I checked my account. The balance had gone from $0 to $6000. Then God spoke to me.

Regarding the issue of faith and support, there are three categories that people will fall into: the Critics, the Crowd, and the Circle.

1. The Critic

This person is driven by selfish and adversarial motives. They will never support you. They may not blatantly say they want you to fail, but their words and actions will prove that they don't want you to succeed-at least not beyond their capability or control. They are never the ones to extend a hand up but are the first ones that, if you fail, will say to you "I told you so". The critic will always find something negative to speak against any decision you make in faith in an effort to stop you from progressing therein. The reason they do this is because your faith either intimidates, challenges, or exposes something in them that is, itself, underdeveloped. The critic is a victim of their own pride and insecurities and, as was mentioned in the previous chapters on the matters, pride and insecurities don't allow us to grow. When I told you about my issues with not being able to celebrate people whose movement in the kingdom threatened my own; that was me being a critic. I didn't support their ministry efforts or invest in their kingdom business or even pat them on the back because it made feel diminished in my identity, my gift, and my faith. (Note: This realization caused me to really look at myself differently, which brought about repentance. I had to go and personally inbox people and tell them I honored them for their accomplishments and was inspired by the things they had done. Don't just move from the place of insecurity, but defeat it by turning it around and using it as inspiration to do better).

The best thing about the critic is that they are pretty easily identified. You know who they are in your life. On the same token, sometimes it's who they are in our lives that hurts us the most. Some people have critics in the form of spiritual coverings who, instead of cultivating the gifts inside of you, are retarding said gifts because they feel threatened. Some of us have critics in the form of parents or loved ones who don't want to see us flourish because of the opportunities that they let pass by.

Whatever the case, we know we have them. Don't expect support. Next, there is:

2. The Crowd

The crowd is much different than the critic because it is filled with people who have no preference to support or not support us. Actually, they don't have too much a preference about anything. The crowd has what I call H_2O= Here to Only Observe. The most prevalent characteristic in the crowd is that they are here to see what's going to happen. They are spectators at most, with no investment in you. They only want to see what's going to happen. They are followers of "people" but it's based solely on the benefit of the actions. In other words, those in the crowd will determine their support of you based on whether or not they can benefit from whatever you're doing. Think about this: when Jesus asked his disciples in Matthew 16 "who do people say I am?", He had already preached on the mount, fed five thousand twice, performed miracles, healed, set free, and delivered and all of that great stuff. Yet, their response to him was, "some say Elijah, some say Moses or one of the other prophets", indicates that some people who were in the crowd following him didn't even know who Jesus was.

You can expect the support of the crowd members as long as you're doing something that benefits them. The crowd will walk with you, watch you, wait for you, but will not be willing to do anything more that demands of them. Lastly, there is:

3. The Circle

Another type of person whose support may seem shaky is not found in the crowd, but the circle. It's the one who loves and cares about us and, because of that devotion, never wants to see us broken. For anyone who has a heart connection to someone else, it's difficult to watch them go through hard times, and even more when it seems as though their own decision is what made it happen. For me, I knew this would be tough. Before I put in my two weeks', I had long conversations with those in my circle who I knew were so connected to me because my struggle would affect them in some way or another. I spoke with my mother first, because, duh, that's what you should do. She had just recently left her job to start a business, and her faith was something I quietly admired and loudly supported. She didn't ask me why, she didn't tell me to go pray about it again. She said she trusted me in hearing God and said however she could support me in this time, she would. (God, I love my mom.) I spoke with my spiritual sisters, Le and AJ. I prefaced our conversations with, "I know what you're going to tell me", sort of as a disclaimer. But, much to my chagrin, they acknowledged my relationship with God and said they'd be praying for me during this time. But, it's not always that easy. Everybody doesn't know the extent of your relationship with God, and while you can tell them of how you've prayed and how God responded and all the details, they will still have their doubts based on their own experiences and their own faith. Hear me and spare yourself some frustration. It is impossible to talk faith with someone who doesn't know the language. When people haven't adopted for themselves a "faith beyond", or haven't given themselves over to a life living blindfolded; it is very hard for them to see and understand, in faith, for someone else.

Again, these people naturally want us to avoid the discomforts of life at all costs and, with the best of intentions, usually will do what they feel is beneficial for us telling us how to get around the pits and potholes when they have the opportunity. But, what if that pit is part of your process? Some people won't be able to see this because, again, they aren't privy to the particulars of your process. They will try to come up with solutions to get you to avoid the places and situations that aren't comfortable. There's a song that my mother used to sing by Regina Belle that comes to mind called "If I Could" (listen to it if you get a chance) and the lyrics are simply the plea of a mother to be able to guard and protect her child from all the pains and tribulations that would come. Sometimes, those in the circle don't understand that these trials of life are necessary for our faith's development and these places, though tough, are the very places that God is using to perfect the purpose in us and prepare us for its greatest performance.

Consider Christ, himself. After three years with his disciples, I think it's safe to say they formed quite a bond. Matthew 16:21 tells of the account. "From that time Jesus began to show to His disciples that He must go to Jerusalem, and suffer many things from the elders and chief priests and scribes, and be killed, and be raised again the third day. Then Peter took Him aside and began to rebuke Him, saying, 'far be it from You, Lord; this shall not happen to You!". How intense is this? Peter, who we know loved Christ (ready to kill for him), spoke against the will of God, even to the point of rebuking Christ the bible says. Peter wasn't being negative or contrary, but he was driven by the same love for Christ and acted as he did because his intention was not to see Christ hurt. I believe that some people won't be able to support you to the level of investment you'd want or expect BECAUSE they love you so much. Let that sink in. Some people, because of their love for you will have a hard time supporting you in your process. Love has a hard time sitting still and having to watch imminent pain. Ask God, who couldn't even watch his son hang on the cross compelling Christ to yell out in agony "Father, Father! Why have you forsaken me?" (Matthew 27:46). While you walk this path of faith, it will seem as though some of your team has forsaken you. But you have to know that God will be with you, even when no one else is able to watch, to do, or to understand. If God called you to the valley, surely, He will be there. If He leads you to a pit, then, surely, he will be there, too. With you. David said in Psalm 139:8 "If I make my bed in hell, behold, You are there."

I believe wholeheartedly the person who gave me their harsh perspective of my situation loves me and cares about my general welfare. I can't say that I didn't understand the concern or the place from which the words were coming. But, the problem was, as hard as this place had become for me and as frustrating as it made me, this was the instruction of God to me. Part of the issue with the walk of faith as a spectator is that they are never as privy to the details of the engagement as are the participants. Being on the outside looking in will only allow one to see the process as it is played out, without hearing the inner workings of the actual process, itself. Think about it, when you sit down and watch your favorite sports team play, you aren't included in on the huddles.

You aren't invited to the team meetings to understand the specifics of the game plan. You don't get to hear what the coach's detailed direction is for the next play. Nope. You only get to watch. Whether you understand it or not, agree to it or not; you're limited in your knowledge of what's going on beyond what you see. The same happens with the spectators of this process in lives. They aren't going to be able to fully understand what's happening because they are restricted in their involvement. They will have their opinions based on what they see, but you have to continue to move based on what you know.

The question you must ask yourself is "am I willing to go alone?" Is your faith really yours if it's only active in the presence and with the affirmation of others? What does it say to God when you believe HIM only if someone else believes YOU? Are you confident and secure enough in your relationship with the Father, that you are able to be like Jairus the synagogue leader whose daughter was dying, and tell the crowd to stay put, put your close circle out of the house, and be still and believe that God alone is who He said He was (Matthew 9:18-26)? Will you be able to, like Peter, sit in a boat in the middle of a sea storm with people you have a connection with and, despite their failure to move with you, step out of the "security" of the boat onto the tumultuous insecurity of the waters all in response to a God that you see and hear out on the ocean? Your faith has to move you beyond what support you may or may not have. Unlike the other moments, this one is more personal and more defining than any other before it. This is the moment that YOUR FAITH becomes the example. This is the moment where you are not speaking for the team or representing the party. This moment is all about you and God; no one else.

Time to READ
REFLECTION EVALUATION ADMISSION DECISION

R-eflection

What initial thoughts and/or emotions did you encounter while reading this chapter? Name and explore them in connection with this idea of having support.

E-valuation

Is your faith in a thing greater influenced by support or not? How do you cope with lack of personal support? Consider those closest to your life, identify them as part of the circle, crowd, or critics. How do you determine the intent of those who may not "support" a decision of yours?

A-dmission

Is it more or less difficult for you to believe in faith while standing alone versus with the support of others? Are you willing to go alone if you had to? Are you afraid to believe alone? If so, why?

D-ecision

What things need to happen in your life (and within your control) and what action steps will you take towards those directives in order for you to learn to live beyond having support?

11- SEEING BEYOND *WAITING*

It was March 25, 2015; and I had just left from the gym; had a pretty good workout session. It had been an interesting time. I was still unemployed, and still searching. I had stumbled across a few great opportunities that I thought would fit me perfectly. Applied to some communication manager or publication specialist positions at area churches basically doing what I do for church and other organizations now but getting paid to do so. However, nothing came through…at least nothing as of yet. So, needless to say, I had become pretty anxious and, in that, more frustrated. It seemed as though nothing was working 'for my good' as the scripture says. And the more I thought about it on this rather short ride home from the gym, the more I realized I had grown truly discontent and dissatisfied with where I was and the condition in which I was found.

I am a doer. If you are reading this book, I'm going to assume that you are as much a doer as I am. Faith takes doing, and well, if you've gotten this far in the book, then you are committed to developing your faith which means you are committed to doing. I, personally, cannot keep still. I am always thinking, always creating; always trying to figure out some way to do something that needs to be done. I don't wait for others to do something if it's within my own power to do. I don't like to sit around and I hate when my ability to do, and do for myself, is compromised or prohibited. One of the main reasons I hate being sick is simply because it requires me to STOP doing in order to get well. So, it takes me longer to get well sometimes because I stubbornly stay doing even when I shouldn't be. With that being said, one of the hardest things in the world for doers like us is having to wait idly for another to do what we have don't have the power or ability to do ourselves. It's called dependence, and it makes us wait with no alternatives, no options, and no other choice. I. Hate. It.

But, that's where I was (or am). I found myself caught in the web of waiting. Now, waiting on God while preoccupied with life wasn't always an issue. I got saved in 2003, October 17 to be exact. I had been serving diligently in ministry since January 2004. I knew God, I had accepted his son as my Lord and savior, and received the indwelling of the Holy Spirit. I didn't have this crazy expectation that every issue would go away. I had struggles, I had financial issues, I had self-image problems, and self-esteem struggles...but I was in a place where none of those things took charge over me (or so I thought). I was content, and "at peace". But things changed. Here it was 2015 and it just hit me while driving that I had lost the peace and will in waiting and hadn't been truly content in maybe ten years. I had grown tired of waiting, and it started to show.

The waiting game is REAL...and despite its name, it isn't much of a game at all. There is nothing fun or enjoyable about it. It's dreadful. It is a patience-building, faith-proving trial of endurance that brings out what's in us, shows it to us, and says now work on it the meantime. It's such an ultimate test of faith because you have to solely rely on an external agent to bring about something which directly affects you. That's scary, and the longer it takes, the more uneasy and unsettled one becomes in the situation.

I was disturbed with the realization of how unhappy I was with life. It hurt to be so discouraged with what I saw. Daily, I was reminded of how gruesome the waiting period was and how deeply unsatisfied I was while there. I didn't get it, and I am not sure that I cared to; I just know that I had no desire to be where I was. The more I thought about it, the more I started to realize how long I had been waiting. The revelation brought about even MORE frustration which eventually became anger. Do you know how torturous it is to be sitting and waiting on promises to be fulfilled while others around you are prospering far beyond what you can imagine? Or how disheartening it is to have to wake up every day to the same realities over which you have no control? Or how about dealing with the conflict that wages inside of you between how great you think you are and how broken you are reflected within your circumstances? It's tough. The longer I waited, the more distant I felt from the promises themselves. It was as though every day, I was one step further away from the life I wanted. Every day I was that much further from what I thought I deserved; from catching up to the people around me who seemed to be enjoying the blessings I wanted to enjoy; from what I believed life should look like for me. I was drifting away from what was prophesied to me about my future. Every day that I played the waiting game, I was one more day behind. While I don't know when exactly the shift from content to discontent came, I do know it happened and I think now I understand why.

In John chapter 11, when Lazarus fell ill, his sisters Martha and Mary sent for their friend Jesus who was about two days away walking time. Lazarus was only sick at the time when Jesus got the message; sick, but alive. The bible tells us that upon getting news about Lazarus' illness, Jesus waited to leave. By the time he had finally arrived, Lazarus was deceased. Not only was Lazarus dead, but he had been buried for four days. Martha and Mary, grieving the loss of their brother, heard the news that Jesus had made it to town. "If you had been here, my brother would not have died!" Martha says begrudgingly to Christ expressing her evident disdain with his timing. See, I was in the same place as Martha. I felt as though I could deal with the situation as long as things didn't get too critical, I could stand to wait. However, it seemed as if God was idly waiting to move on my behalf, causing the life and hope that I had in the promises to fade, just slightly, day by day. And, I don't know how long you've been waiting for whatever God has promised you but, take it from me, after some time, your patience runs low, your expectations grow dim, and your hope fades as you live in the daily reality of what is. My cry to God was always "what are you waiting for?" thinking that I had it all together and He was the holdup. But, I found out that the real question should have been "why am I waiting?"

Our waiting on God has a few different purposes. We know one, it's blatant.

1. **Waiting proves our integrity through patience.**

The bible states it very clearly in Hebrews 10 that there is a need for patience. A need to suffer? Sure! For how can we reign with a God with whom we haven't suffered? Think about it, do you really trust people who get going when things get tough, and come back when they are better? Do you really trust those people who are one way in the sunshine and another way when the pressure of the storm comes? Waiting allows for patience to prove us and show that we are indeed of the fabric we claim. We need it, so that the integrity of our faith, our confession, and our profession can be made sure.

So, He makes us wait. Fine, that's easy to understand. Luckily, the second one isn't too hard, either.

2. Waiting equips and prepares us for something ahead.

He's preparing you for what has already been prepared *for* you. Truth is, what's spoken for your life is already in motion, but we have to do more than just get there! We have to arrive to these blessings and these promises in a condition that doesn't put at risk their successful manifestation and implementation in our lives. Consider this: if you ever played sports, you know the strenuous schedule of practice is all but fun. However, the coach would be a fool to show up to the field of the opponent and not have had you prepared to play. Waiting is a process that helps to equip and prepare us to not just show up, but to be effective when we do. But, there's another reason as to why we wait, and I believe it has everything to do with our faith.

Now, as I mentioned before, faith can only be as strong and certain as that in which it is placed. We don't go around bragging confidently about the things we aren't sure about. So it is with our faith.

3. Waiting helps to change our perception of, and thus increase our confidence in, God.

I was guilty of perceiving God as needing circumstances in His favor to work them out in mine. *Never allow your situation to have the power of limitation over your aspirations and expectations.*

Keep in mind that perception affects actions. If I perceive that you're a thief, I won't have you around too many things that I consider valuable. How we perceive something ultimately determines the degree and manner in which we interact with it and all things we associate with it. Faith is action, and just like any other action, it is heavily influenced and shaded by perception. While there is nothing wrong with that alone, it is when we allow the perception of situations to affect our interactions with God negatively do issues occur. The longer we are made to wait, the more our focus shifts from the sovereignty of God to the severity of our circumstances.

Perception always influences interactions, and so when we adopt a negative perception it will have a negative effect on how we operate within the scheme of things relative. This is the challenge in waiting...being able to do so without becoming pessimistic. The hard part is that the longer we have to endure the wait, usually the greater the possibility that we can lose some of our optimism and hope. Waiting itself wasn't the issue of my disdain...it was the length of time that I was made to wait and how

I viewed it. Waiting is not the problem, it's waiting beyond what we expected that presents potential dangers to our faith. We all have waited, and possess some level of patience to do so. But, it's when the wait takes longer than we prepared for when we encounter difficulty. It's at that point that we start to view waiting as uncomfortable and an inconvenience; the moment that it becomes a thorn. It's when the waiting makes us feel as though we aren't being considered that the problem arises. It's when the resources no longer meet the demands and we start lacking that we become worried and switch our focus. It's when the patience starts running thin and we aren't responding the same way that the waiting poses its most vital threat.

I had adopted a negative perception towards God because of my waiting. Now, I know what the crowd is going to say. This whole rhetoric about Christians not seeking happiness because it dependent upon what's happening, and how we shouldn't be dictated by our circumstances. I mean, I get it. I really do. Joy is what we seek because it is a fruit of the spirit, and well circumstances should not dictate our attitudes or dispositions. Yeah, yeah, Blah, blah. Can we be honest? We are human, y'all, and creatures of circumstance. Maybe not always directly, intentionally, or even consciously; but to think that we as Christians are void of our natural disposition of being human is faulty, at best. Faulty, because what this type of "avoidance" does is make us try to ignore and essentially live in a place of denial as it relates to our emotional state of content, or discontent rather. I think the problem is the definitions of happiness that we have adopted into our thinking.

I read something once that said God is not concerned with whether you have success in life (be it in relationships, wealth, business, personal ambitions and goals, etc.) It purported that our sole purpose, and thus the aim of our existence, is to bring God glory and to be settled with however it looks. Now, let me make this clear: I am completely in agreement with the fact that our lives are to be used as platforms for God's glory. We are vessels and we are here to live for God. My question, I guess, comes at the claim that God is not concerned about HOW we go through this life.

I, like a good ol' Christian, had adopted this mindset that God isn't worried about my happiness, and as long as I had Him, I should be satisfied with whatever place I found myself. I tried that for ten years, and as I sat in that car almost in tears, I concluded that it did nothing but made me passive and bitter within my relationship with God. This idea that God wasn't interested in how I went through life made me hesitant to bring my unhappiness to God's attention. If God is not concerned about my condition, emotional state, or how I was making it through, then why would I bring it up in prayer? This ideology forces us to ignore parts of us that are both very real and that contribute to our overall disposition and countenance. It creates a numbness, that after you ignore for a while, brings a silent resentment that, while you may not admit it, know it is there. This false premise restricts the relationship with God, because makes me feel as if He's only concerned about me as it relates to Him. This teaching is not biblical neither is it productive in the progression of intimacy with God. Listen to me, God cares. 1 Peter 5:7 tells us to place all our cares on Him, because He cares for us. God doesn't just want you to arrive in your place of destiny, but He wants you to arrive in a condition that allows you to be productive, passionate, and purposeful in that place.

Time to READ
REFLECTION EVALUATION ADMISSION DECISION

R-eflection

What initial thoughts and/or emotions did you encounter while reading this chapter? Name and explore them in connection with this idea of having to wait.

E-valuation

What's your general attitude around waiting and why? Discuss: do you ever feel like you have been waiting longer than you should have? Consider a time where you had to wait (faith): How were you proven in the wait? How were your prepared/equipped in the wait? How did your perceptions changed during the period of waiting?

A-dmission

What are you still waiting on OR what have you stopped waiting for? What are you doing while you wait? Do you believe God is concerned with how you journey through life? Have you ever moved too soon in a thing? If so, how would have waiting benefitted you?

D-ecision

What things need to happen in your life (and within your control) and what action steps will you take towards those directives in order for you to learn to live beyond the period of waiting?

12- SEEING BEYOND *RESULTS*

So, there I was. I had become a zombie. I felt displaced, as if I was in transit. I was packed up emotionally and spiritually, and had become empty, with all of my substance in scattered boxes. I was waiting for God to do something that would blow my mind away and make sense of the entire act of faith...and nothing. I had grown restless, and eventually, stoic. It was evident. At my home church, I withdrew from my attachment. Didn't intend to, but it happened. I was a shell; there but not at all present. Emotionally, I was all over the place. Up one day, down the next. I wanted to cry, but couldn't. I wanted to scream, but didn't. I was overwhelmed, and being taken through a gauntlet of feelings. I was frustrated. I was sad. I was disappointed. Spiritually, I seemed to be missing something, but I couldn't put my finger on it. Things had shifted and were different. My worship changed, my desire changed. I had no idea what was going on, but I was certain it had everything to do with this process.

I knew this would be a year of transition and, couple that with the stepping out in faith, I allowed my imagination to direct my expectations into a much different result. But, nothing had unfolded as I had expected. I was doing my best not to become angry with God, but my best was proving not to be good enough. With every passing day of the same reality and failure to see the results of my act of faith as I had envisioned, I became more and more discontent and disconnected. It perpetuated the state of displacement I was feeling and, get this, I began to doubt that initial act of faith was ever God-driven at all. I was confused, and confusion for me leads to frustration. Frustration without answers leads to discouragement which usually leads me to isolation and, eventually, depression and destruction (behavior that doesn't build me in any positive way). I didn't get it. I listened, in faith; obeyed in faith; despite the naysayers, I went with it, in faith…and no reward. So, I took a few deep breaths in an effort to mask my anger, and I questioned God. "You said that you would reward those who diligently sought you…where's my reward? I've been waiting, where's my reward that I've been seeking? I stepped out, I trusted you. Why would lead me to leave me…I'm drowning. Where are you?"

God began to speak to me. In pieces, He spoke, and eventually, it all came together. First, He spoke on the issue of waiting. I mentioned in the last chapter how I was playing this waiting game because, well from October to what was now June, that's all I was doing. Here's the issue God pointed out to me in my "waiting": I was getting tired. Y'all, I was ready to quit. I was giving up. These are not the indications that the word gives for those who are waiting on the Lord. Isaiah declared that "But they that wait upon the Lord shall renew their strength; they shall mount up with wings as eagles; they shall run, and not be weary; and they shall walk, and not faint." (40:31) If, in our waiting on God, we find ourselves losing strength, feeling depressed and discouraged, growing weary and giving up; then we aren't "waiting" on God as He would define. It is in these cases where we are the ones on whom God is waiting, not the other way around.

When God is waiting on us, that means it's our move. For me, it should've been writing this book, but I was too busy trying to put myself back in the same situation from which I had just asked God to deliver me. Fine, God's waiting on me. Still didn't make much sense because I felt I was doing all I could on my part. I was putting in applications, daily. No bites. From anywhere. If, in the rare instance, I would get a response, it would only fall through based off some random premise. So, I asked again. "Where's my reward. What are you waiting for? What do you want from me?" And, again, He speaks. This time, about my expectation, my faith; and I wasn't ready for this one. Very clearly He says YOU NEED TO CHANGE YOUR FAITH. Here's what happened, that often happens with us. *WE MISAPPROPRIATE OUR FAITH*. Instead of placing our faith in God's being (himself), we wrongly place our faith in God's DOING. When we make the mistake of doing this, our hope (that thing which our faith substantiates) is built on the contingency of God's action; which, if we're being honest, is usually something driven by our own desires and selfish expectations. I have to be very careful in explaining this as it was given to me, so bear with me a little.

What I don't want is anyone to confuse the fact that I believe God wants to bless us and that He is concerned about what concerns us. Yes, we have scriptures that support our being able to ask in faith for God to do, and Him honoring what we ask (in accordance with His will). That's not what I'm debating here.

What I'm discussing is what we do, almost subconsciously, when it comes to this expectation. If we aren't intentionally careful in the placement our faith, those actions can literally stall the move of God in our lives.

Let's remember faith pleases God, Hebrews 11:6 teaches us so well. But, think about why? At the core of true faith is not only belief but also obedience, and the scripture lets us know what should be the motivation of this God-pleasing faith. "They that come, must come believing that he is God and that He is a rewarder of those who seek HIM". Not once does the scripture mention what you believe God to DO; however, multiple times does it highlight a faith that believes and focuses on GOD himself. If your motivation to act in response to God's urging is SOLELY and PRIMARILY based on the premise that God may do for you in response, then you have nothing more than a "conditional faith". Conditional faith says "I'm only doing this because God's going to do (insert action here)." Conditional faith is not true faith, and we must be careful of adopting and operating in the former, and here's why.

1. This kind of faith is dangerous to the health of your relationship with God.

When we operate in this manner, we end up giving God the condition to which we will obey him in faith. It's often extremely latent but very real and very prevalent, and without even trying we make what should please God about what God can do to please us. In a moment, without even trying, we move from worship to manipulation. We say things like "Ok God, if you do ......, then

I'll …" or "God, I'm going to …. But you must …." It doesn't even seem bad, right? I said it myself. "God, I'm gonna trust you and leave this job and you must have a better job lined up for me". Innocently, I spoke this, and have been looking for the better job since. Again, I'm not saying that God won't bless you for your faith, I'm saying that your faith shouldn't be motivated by the blessing but rather by obedience to the authority and person of God. What if God doesn't come in the way in which you mandated through your expectation? The bible says that hope deferred makes the heart sick, and I can attest that nothing is more discouraging and disheartening than when you feel as though God is not with you or for you (see chapter 9). When everything you're asking for is being dashed to pieces right in front of you, and you're being denied the very things you've been praying for, it is spirit crushing and creates a wedge between you and God. Unanswered prayer usually causes us to stop praying after a while. Unfulfilled hope usually leads to us ceasing in our expectations after a while. Disappointments usually lead us to look elsewhere (often within our own means) to make something happen. When our faith is conditional upon our expectation, if God's will doesn't agree to our will, we usually find ourselves (unfairly) at odds with him. Secondly:

2. This kind of faith limits your perspective on the plans of God.

When your hope is built on the expectation; that's all you'll end up looking for: the tangible product. Instead of recognizing and appreciating what God is doing, you're growing bitter because of frustration with what you feel God isn't doing or hasn't done.

There I was waiting for God to give me a "better job" that I almost missed what God was doing in my life that was both praiseworthy and worth being celebrated. How many times have you been so concerned with and consumed by your own stuff that you missed the blessing of God? How many times did you play Martha when you should've been playing Mary?

When God gave me the instructions to leave the job, He simultaneously gave me directives to become more involved on my campus, which I did. I started interning in the Office of Student Affairs and with the Coordinator of Student Conduct, Thomasina Boardley, in the administration building. I volunteered time with the SGA and Student Life offices; gave a lot more energy to the campus ministry and the growth of its members; and, I made myself available for the mentoring of others. In the time of my complaining and grumbling because God hadn't delivered in the way I selfishly expected, here's what God HAD done. He had allowed me to make intimate connections with every single administrative personnel at the University, including the president at the time, Dr. Mickey Burnim. They each knew me by name. He made it so that I would become extremely close with the VP of Student Affairs, Dr. Artie Travis, being called on by him to assist he and his team in identifying needs and creating solutions for the improvement of student experience on campus. He gave me the honor of becoming a mentor and mediator for male students on the campus. Because of him, I was handpicked by the Chief of Staff of the University President to work on the revitalization of the campus-wide Male Initiative, and given free reign to help restructure and redesign that effort which has become a mainstay of the campus culture. He blessed me immensely by giving me student aid, scholarships, and access to opportunities I neither applied nor asked for. I was even invited to sit on a council of about fifteen with the County Police Chief and his Deputy Chiefs, Inspector General, and other administrative leaders. That's just a small glimpse at the much greater picture of God's handiwork that showed up in intangible ways throughout and far reaching beyond my time at Bowie.

When you, like I, become preoccupied with what YOU WANT God to do; you, like I, will subsequently miss out on all that GOD WANTS to do. I don't know much, but what I do know is God is able to do exceedingly above all that I could ever ask or think. His plans are always better than mine. This is why the psalmist advises us to delight ourselves in the PERSON of God, alone, and He will give us what we are to desire (Psalm 37:4). Next:

3. This type of faith will hinder your process of maturation and development.

Conditional faith is both inconsistent and convenient, which means it only holds up within conditions deemed favorable by the holder. Such faith can't be trusted because anything that is inconsistent in its integrity will fail to produce consistent results when tested. The bible teaches us in the book of Peter that the testing of our faith will indeed come by fire. Faith is always tested in order to be proven. Think about this, though, if faith has to be proven, that should let you know that there is some type of imposter faith in existence out there. Paul tells us in Romans that these trials of our faith work to develop our patience, which has the responsibility of perfecting us (James 1). Conditional faith lacks the components of true faith and therefore, won't produce from the trial what true faith would yield. No production equals no patience, which leads to us remaining incomplete.

4. This kind of faith subverts God's authority in your life.

If true faith is what it takes to please God, then the contrary of one has to mean the contrary of the other. Lack of true faith not only displeases God, but it keeps him from responding in the manner in which He prefers. When we operate in this manipulative way, we place what we want above what God wants, acting only when it serves to please us. Imagine if you had a child to whom you were a sufficient parent. You feed them, house them, clothe them, and make sure they have a pretty decent life, even it means sacrificing of yourself. Now, imagine giving that same child some basic instructions such as cleaning their room or respecting the household curfew, something simple. Instead of obeying with regard to who you are as their parent, provider and source; they respond with, "well what are you going to do for me for doing it?" This is exactly what we don't want God to feel, but conditional faith will cause this to happen. We must be able to respond to God with faith that is found in obedience to WHO HE IS not how we can benefit. When we think like that child, we reverse the order of worship and sovereignty by making God serve us in the manner in which we deem is acceptable. God will NEVER respond favorably to the motive that displaces his lordship for our selfish pleasures.

Consider the three Hebrew boys and the faith they had to display at the moment the horn was sounded and they were to bow and worship the image of King Nebuchednezzar. Faced with the punishment of being burned alive in the furnace of fire, they didn't say "God I have faith that you will deliver me from this furnace SO I will not bow and jump in." Their faith was found in who God was and their testimony and declaration made that evident. They didn't bow because of their obedience and respect to their God and his law (wishes), and when faced with the repercussions, they said "Our God is able to deliver us from this, but even if he doesn't, he is still able". True faith in action says I'm going to do this because of who God is; and, even if he does nothing in response, He is still God and my faith is still resting steadfast in Him and Him alone.

Faith beyond the act moves us to obey no matter what may or may not come as a result. It allows us to endure even the toughest of times because it is planted in who God is. It gives us joy in the midst of despair because it is not based on what's happening around us, but rather rooted in who God is. It's how we have peace in the valley experience, because it is not reliant upon on how comfortable our situation is, but rather established in WHO God is. It keeps us calm in the storms of life because it is not dependent upon how fair God has made the weather to be, but rather is grounded in WHO God is. It allows us to face evils with a certain level of confidence. It empowers us not to bow in the face of adversity or take a stand that's only contingent upon God's deliverance. It's how David was able to proclaim the 23rd Psalm, and it's how you and I will be able to successfully make it through to the next place in our lives with God.

Time to READ
REFLECTION EVALUATION ADMISSION DECISION

R-eflection

What initial thoughts and/or emotions did you encounter while reading this chapter? Name and explore them in connection with this idea of expected results.

E-valuation

Have you experienced or ever engaged in acts of faith that have seemed to go unfruitful? When and where has your faith been conditional? Has your faith been a response to God's person or God's doing?

A-dmission

Describe a time you have ever felt abandoned by God mid-process. Has your faith been misappropriated? Have things gone as you expected them to go? How have you responded to failed expectations? Discuss a time where you may have missed what God was doing because you were so focused on what you think He wasn't doing?

D-ecision

What things need to happen in your life (and within your control) and what action steps will you take towards those directives in order for you to learn to live beyond being results?

13- SEEING BEYOND *YOURSELF*

The Concluding Chapter

"Strength" William Murphy

Let me first start this chapter by saying "God is amazing!" I am exhausted dealing with and having been with by this process, but right now at midnight on July 1st, I am so honored and humbled by who God is. It's nothing short of amazing how He allows things to work out for our good. Sometimes, we can still be in the same situation and have a better state of mind; and, going from feeling defeated in your "stuff" to feeling inspired in your "stuff" is always GOOD!

Every night when the process of development got away from what I viewed as my own control, I found myself asking God "where are you?" The frustration increased with time. The confusion set in after a while, and then doubt. There were days when quitting was my only recourse, and I couldn't even do that. I kept asking God the same question. "Where are you?" My bills continued to stack up, my debt to collectors, friends, and family followed the same pattern; and, still there was no answer from God. Hundreds of applications submitted with no response. Two interviews with no follow-up, and my question was still the same-

"God, where are you?" Every plan foiled, and everything that could offer some sense of security was thrown completely out of whack. I was on the water alone, too far out to go back to the boat, yet, too far out too see anything but the winds and waves.

I realized that this process isn't as much about finding out where God is, as much as it is about bringing your attention to where He isn't and why. As long as I kept asking God that question, it was proof that I had adopted the wrong perspective, attitude and mindset toward this experience. I was missing the point of the entire process, and my intentions were set more on God's *intervention* rather than on his *supervision* in my development. Instead of worrying about why I was going through, I was focused on why God had yet to come through. I was missing it, and it was happening right around me. And God remained silent because if I didn't get it this time, I would be forced to endure the hardships of facing this course and learning these lessons all over again. How amazing is that?! God would rather sit silently and let you find the answer than to expose you to such a process a third, fourth, hundredth time. Silence is safety, sometimes. This was not about where God was, this was about finding out where and who I was. In order to get from this what was purposed, I had to see this as something God had ordained for my good. I had to figure out how this was meant to make me better. If your response to God is always from the perspective of "woe is me" instead of counting it all joy, looking for the opportunity to be made better; you have the wrong mindset and aren't ready for new levels. God will never honor the expectation of elevation until we first master the operation of appreciation. What I had to realize was that:

1. Faith isn't a method to prove God, but a method to prove us.

Though the writer of Hebrews had already made mention of it, I was completely focused on myself that I couldn't see what was clearly evident. "Without faith it is impossible to please God. For He that cometh must come knowing that God is and that he is a rewarder of those who diligently seek him." (Heb. 11:6). If faith as about proving God, then how would it also be a factor that produced his pleasure? Furthermore, if faith were about proving God, then this entire scripture would be made invalid. Who seeks after what they don't believe exists? Who follows what they don't hear? Who moves in faith unless they first ALREADY BELIEVE?

Faith isn't about proving God, it's about proving us! God is the one constant in our developmental process of faith, life even. If faith were about us proving God, then the entire process would be in our control. All the circumstance and situations, all the plot twists and turns; they all would be at our beckon and disposal. But that's not how it works as that's not the intent of the processes of faith. We must be proven. It has to be proven to God that the integrity of our substance is able to remain intact through whatever comes our way, good or bad. It needs to be proven that our commitment to our confession is true to the point of action beyond our comfort, for as Paul stated in 1 Corinthians 4, "the Kingdom of God is not in word, but in power" (demonstration, action). It must be proven to our enemy, our naysayers, our opposition, and even ourselves, that we are who God says we are.

I was afraid to write this book. At times, I thought I was crazy and maybe should stop somewhere in the middle, because of the fear that I associated not with the task at hand, but with everything that was on the line. This wasn't about if I could write. I can talk, so having a conversation with the screen while taking dictation wasn't anything major. This was about so much more. For so long, I had convinced myself that I was something special. Even when I struggled with my own self-identity and self-love, or low self-esteem to the point of planning my own death; I was still rather convinced that I was something great. Can you imagine the waves of that internal conflict? Didn't know what or why, and maybe it was those around me who made me buy into it eventually; but, every dream was always BIG, every VISION was always VAST, and I just knew that God had something great planned for me (even if I ignored it). But, there I was at 29 with nothing to support that claim. Sure, I had potential; but little proof. I was un-degreed, unemployed, unable to provide for myself, unmarried (heck, I wasn't even dating), unsuccessful at business with a failed T-shirt venture sitting in my closet collecting dust, unfulfilled and completely UNACCOMPLISHED. There was nothing about what I saw that was congruent with what I believed and I was at odds with if I still believed it or not. I had no evidence, no proof, and nothing substantial to support the claim. This was all I had. This wasn't about writing, this was about proving to me that I was more than what the evidence (or lack thereof) showed. This was life or death in the matter of dreams and hope for anything beyond my now. This was big, and I was afraid. Afraid that maybe I was wrong about it all. Could I have been wrong to think that I was anything more than what my life had shown me? Could I have been wrong to assume that God's plan for my life was more than the current state of struggle?

Maybe this was it; and if so, then I clearly couldn't trust the relationship I thought I had with God. The fear that was attached to this was real, and almost paralyzing. But, here's the thing with fear…it never subsides without action against it. Fear needs to be confronted with faith (action) and I'm not being churchy here, I'm saying in real life, if you don't do SOMETHING in opposition to that fear, you won't ever start believing you are able to do or be ***ANYTHING BEYOND*** what it restricts you to. The one who is bullied lives in fear of the bully UNTIL THEY DECIDE TO STAND UP for themselves. The one who can't swim for fear of the waters will remain on the shores UNTIL THEY DECIDE TO GET IN. Fear takes action to be defeated, and that action is the definition of your faith! It is that action that will prove to you that YOU ARE EVERYHING He said you were. It is that action that will make you a believer and no longer a doubter of your own value, worth, and greatness. It is THAT ACTION which will finally loose you from the grip of fear and move you into the realm of faith beyond. I also had to learn that:

2. God is where your faith is.

In all that panic and hysteria, the fear and doubt…through all of this, every chapter of this book…none of it means anything if you miss the point of a life lived with faith beyond. God pleased by faith and so, naturally, is drawn to ours. So, it's never a question of where GOD is but rather, where your faith is. When our lives are lived with the blindfolds of faith off and we refuse (for whatever reason) to engage God's involvement in our lives; what right do we have to stand in expectation of God's influence and outcomes in our lives? Sure, some of our situations are completely at the discretion of God's hand…but most of our issues are a matter of response, and the truth is we receive based on the system upon which we respond. I had no evidence of my thought of self because, though God initiated processes in my life, I failed to give God room to be involved. I struggled with self-esteem because I kept it private and didn't choose to trust God with it. I may have been unmarried but that was because I dealt with some issues within myself that caused me to remove myself from the process of dating. Again, I didn't give it over to God, completely. It took some admonishing and some redefining of my perspective, but faith gave me proof and proof gave me hope. Yes, I was un-degreed, but faith gave me the insight to understand that God was the only reason I was able to even get back in school, paying a debt I had owed for years and having secured adequate funds to be able to see the end in sight. Yes, I had endured some failures; but through faith, God's insight showed me that I no longer had to internalize that failure as an identity. Yes, I was twenty-nine, and while I kept figuring the glass to be half-empty while time was steadily slipping away, it was faith beyond the norm that finally made me see that life was nowhere near over. Faith reassured me that my future belonged to a God who stood outside of time. Faith caused me to understand that I wasn't unaccomplished, I was just unfinished; and that God was faithful to complete the work He started in me. Faith gave me the power to be patient and the confidence to know that every promise and every purpose for my life was within my reach and within His control.

True lives of faith must go beyond self. As stated in the beginning of this book, we are faith's opposition, so in order to let faith rule we must be willing to relinquish that reign of self. It has to move us beyond US. Beyond our opinions, our fears, our doubts, our hangups. Beyond our failures, beyond our perceptions, beyond our positions, and beyond our disappointments. Faith, because it involves something greater than us, sees beyond what we see and knows beyond what we know. We have to choose to believe in that something to the point of submitting all of who we are to its subjection, authority, and control. If Christ is our example, then let us look to him and adopt his mindset. Paul put it this way:

"Let this same attitude *and* purpose *and* [humble] mind be in you which was in Christ Jesus: [Let Him be your example in humility:[6] Who, although being essentially one with God *and* in the form of God [[b]possessing the fullness of the attributes which make God God], did not[c]think this equality with God was a thing to be eagerly grasped [d]*or* retained,[7] But stripped Himself [of all privileges and [e]rightful dignity], so as to assume the guise of a servant (slave), in that He became like men *and* was born a human being.[8] And after He had appeared in human form, He abased *and* humbled Himself [still further] and carried His obedience to the extreme of death, even the death of the cross! [9] Therefore [because He stooped so low] God has highly exalted Him and has[f]freely bestowed on Him the name that is above every name,[10] That in (at) the name of Jesus every knee [g]should (must) bow, in heaven and on earth and under the earth,[11] And every tongue [[h]frankly and openly] confess *and* acknowledge that Jesus Christ is Lord, to the glory of God the Father." (Phil. 2:5-11)

Adopting this mindset towards faith, or God's supreme involvement in your life as Christ did, will cause us to do as Christ did. Like Christ, it may require redefining our perceptions of self, but it'll be worth it. Like Christ, it may warrant reconsidering our position of self, to give up our inhibitions and our reservations; but it will be worth it. Like Christ, faith may even demand us to release our possession of self, but it will be worth it.

Give yourself over to a world, no, a life of faith in order to become all that God said you are and to see God's intentions for your life show up in the earth. Sure, it will require more of you; but the best of you will always require more of you. The evidence of everything you've hoped for is out there, but it's beyond you, beyond the boat. You're looking with the wrong set of eyes…and until you live blindfolded and are walking by faith, you will keep missing it. But, today, I dare you to find it. And, once you find it, pursue it, and do whatever it takes to live it.

Remember, *your best you should be your only option*.
Godspeed.